ART THERAPY

AN ANTI-STRESS COLOURING BOOK

LOM ART

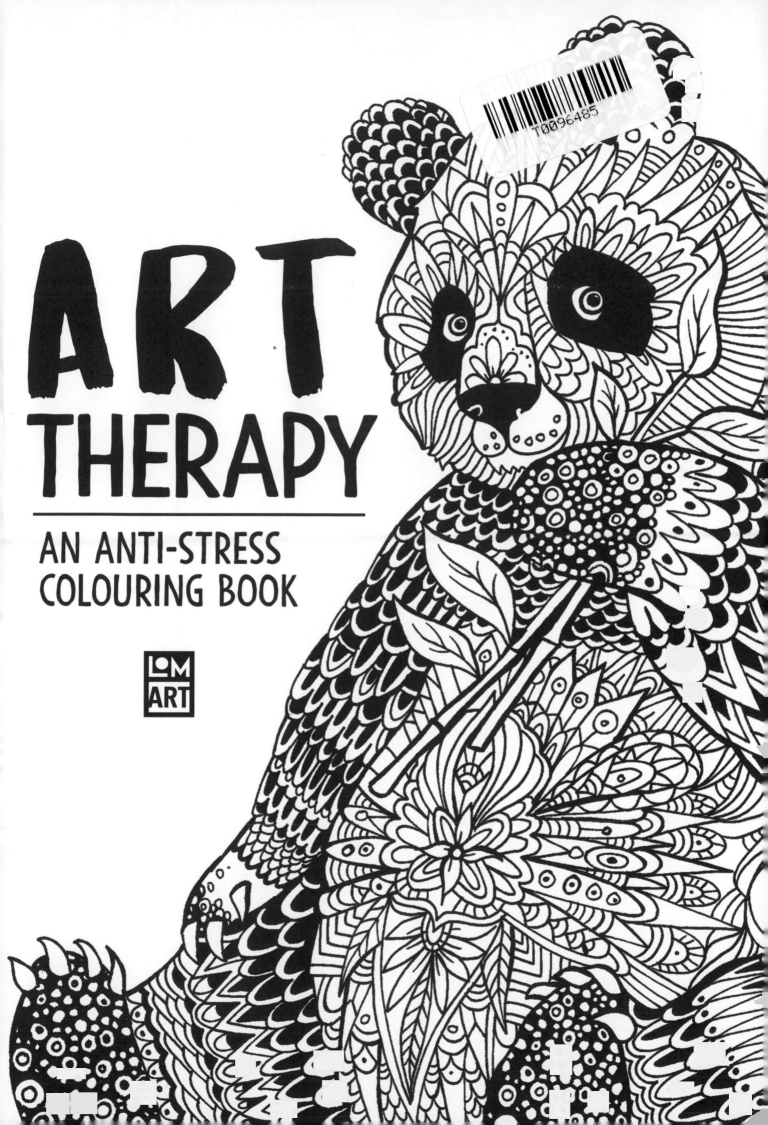

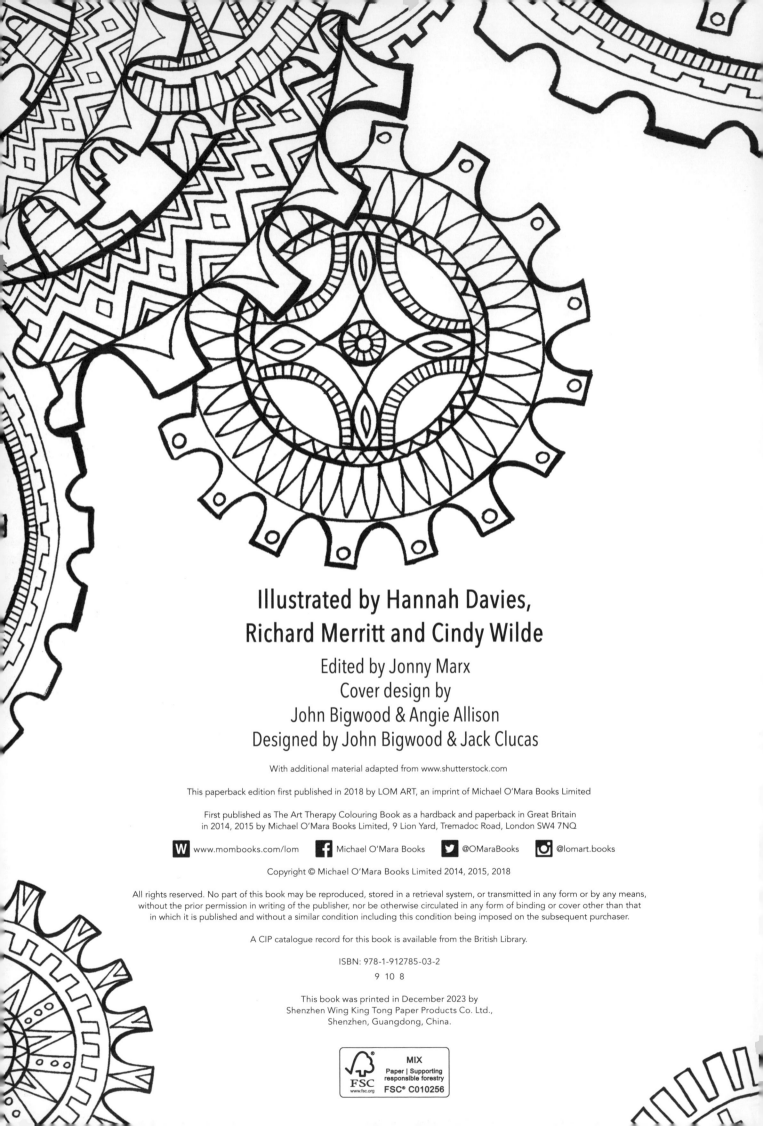

Illustrated by Hannah Davies, Richard Merritt and Cindy Wilde

Edited by Jonny Marx
Cover design by
John Bigwood & Angie Allison
Designed by John Bigwood & Jack Clucas

With additional material adapted from www.shutterstock.com

This paperback edition first published in 2018 by LOM ART, an imprint of Michael O'Mara Books Limited

First published as The Art Therapy Colouring Book as a hardback and paperback in Great Britain
in 2014, 2015 by Michael O'Mara Books Limited, 9 Lion Yard, Tremadoc Road, London SW4 7NQ

W www.mombooks.com/lom   f Michael O'Mara Books   🐦 @OMaraBooks   📷 @lomart.books

A CIP catalogue record for this book is available from the British Library.

ISBN: 978-1-912785-03-2

9 10 8

This book was printed in December 2023 by
Shenzhen Wing King Tong Paper Products Co. Ltd.,
Shenzhen, Guangdong, China.

FSC
www.fsc.org

MIX
Paper | Supporting
responsible forestry
FSC® C010256

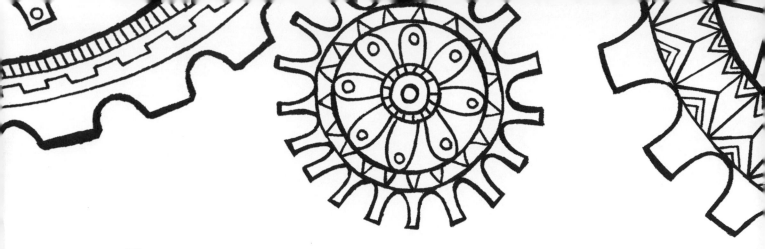

From doodling with loose lines and loops to colouring in complex designs, every activity in this book has been carefully crafted so you can enjoy the satisfaction of creating something beautiful.

With colouring and doodling, you need have no fear of making mistakes or failing. There is no right or wrong technique, only the opportunity to create stunning art. That's why this book contains no rules or complicated step-by-step instructions — you don't even have to stay within the lines if you don't want to.

From magical mandalas and rhythmical repeating patterns to gorgeous geometric designs and free-flowing doodles, the pictures in this book will help unlock your creativity and confidence. They will distract you from the stresses and strains of everyday life, and help you experience the calm that comes from focusing on simple tasks.

Pages for you to colour are at the beginning of the book, and there are doodles to do at the back. So pick up a pen, choose a page you like the look of, and start drawing.

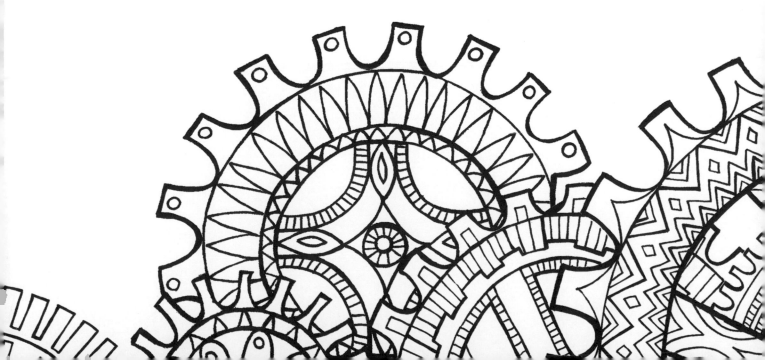

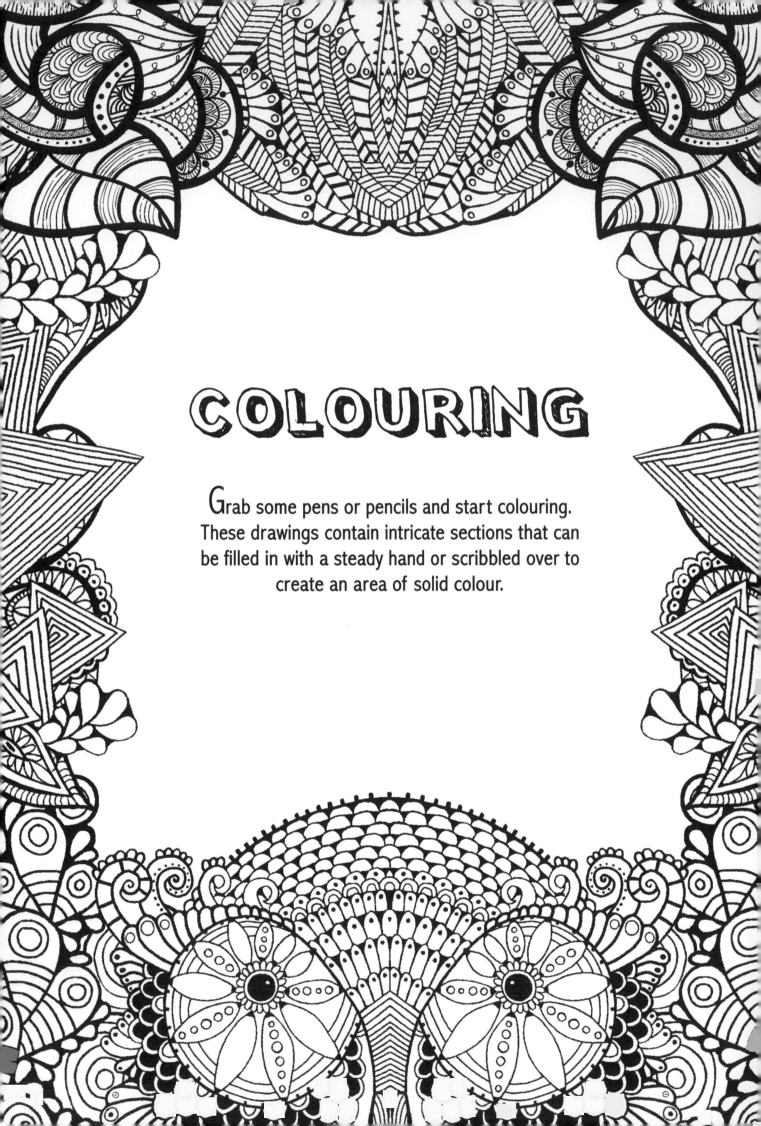

COLOURING

Grab some pens or pencils and start colouring. These drawings contain intricate sections that can be filled in with a steady hand or scribbled over to create an area of solid colour.

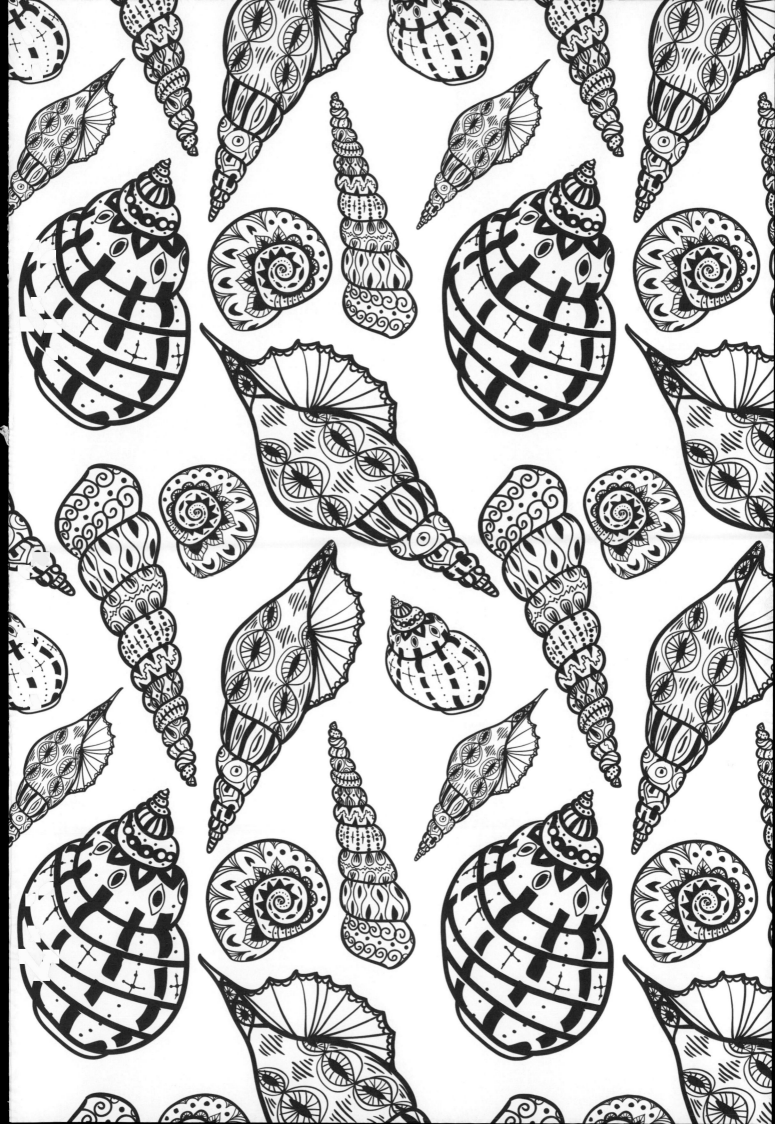

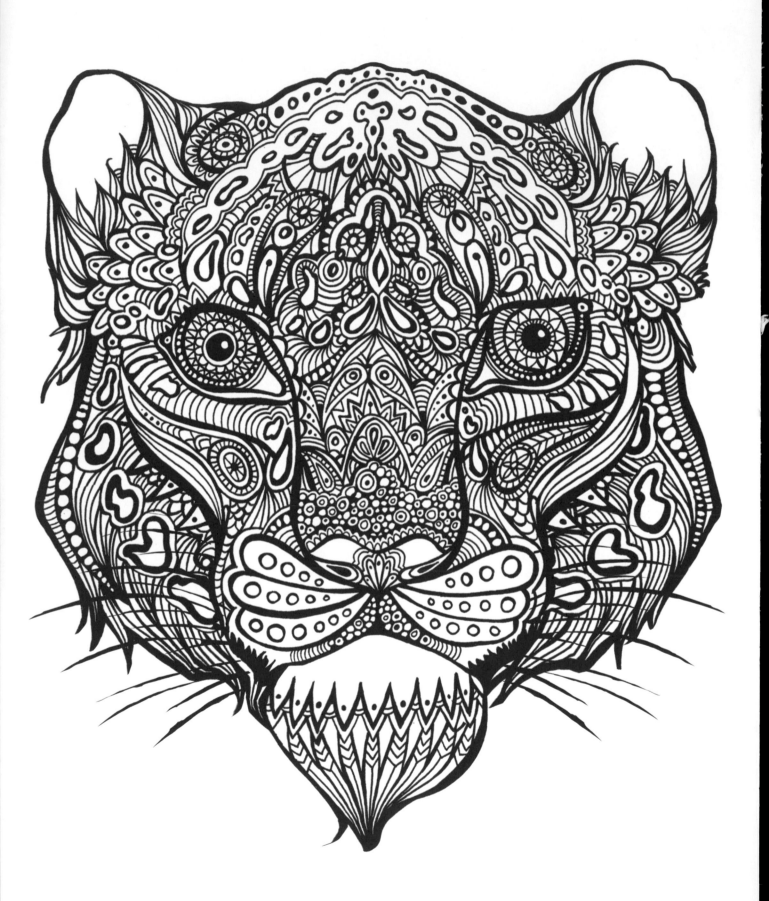

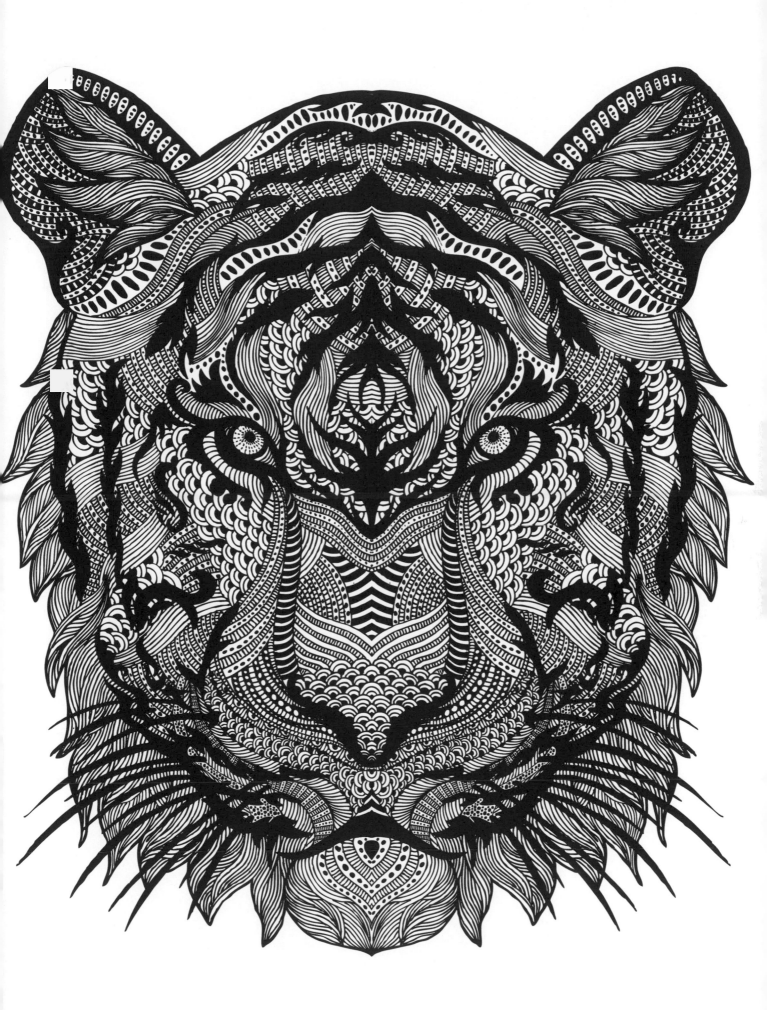

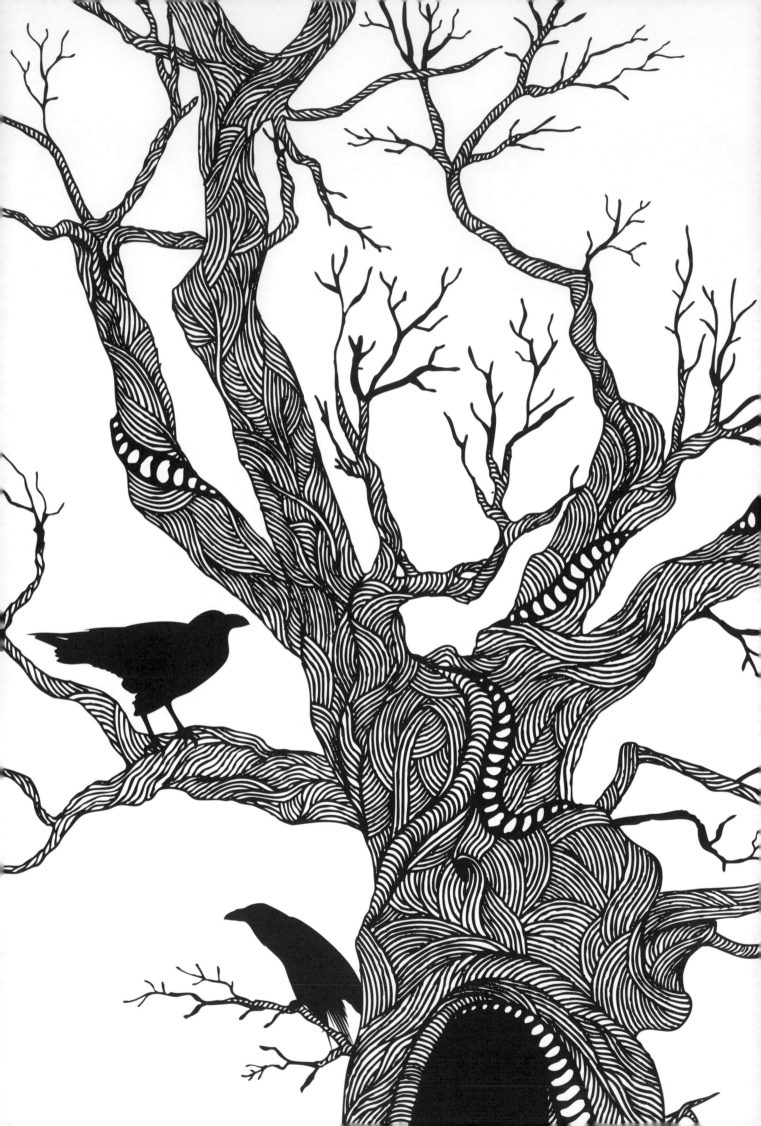

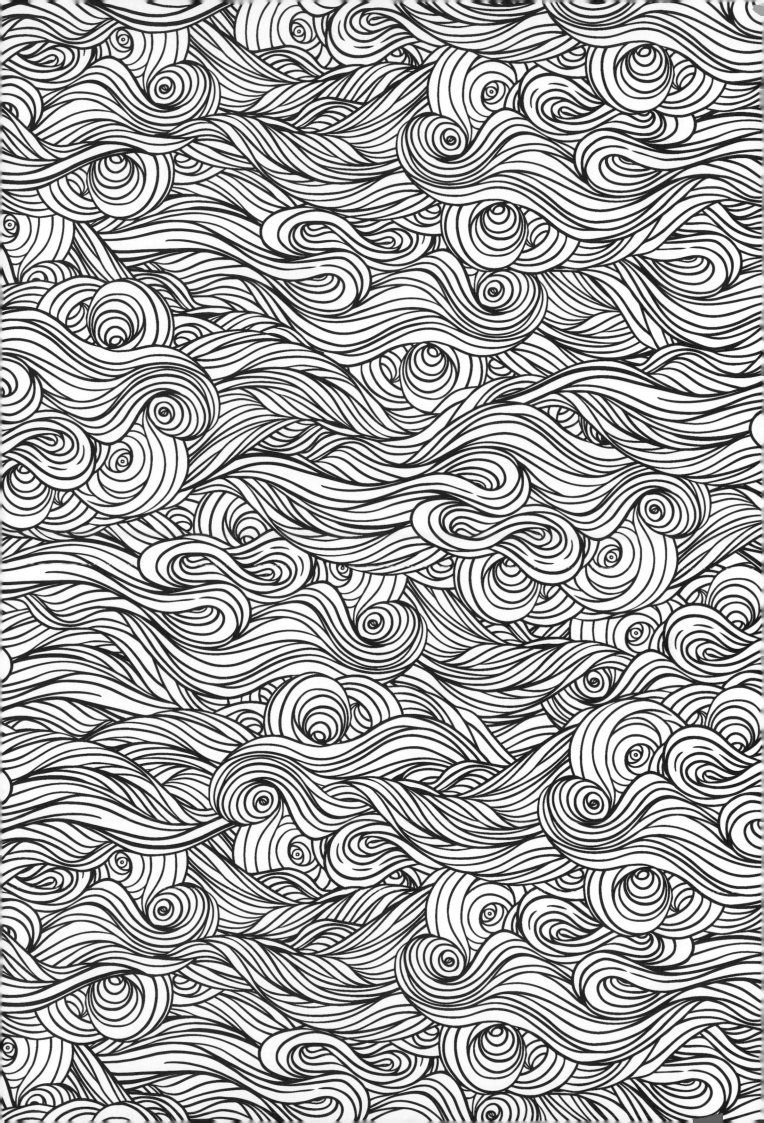

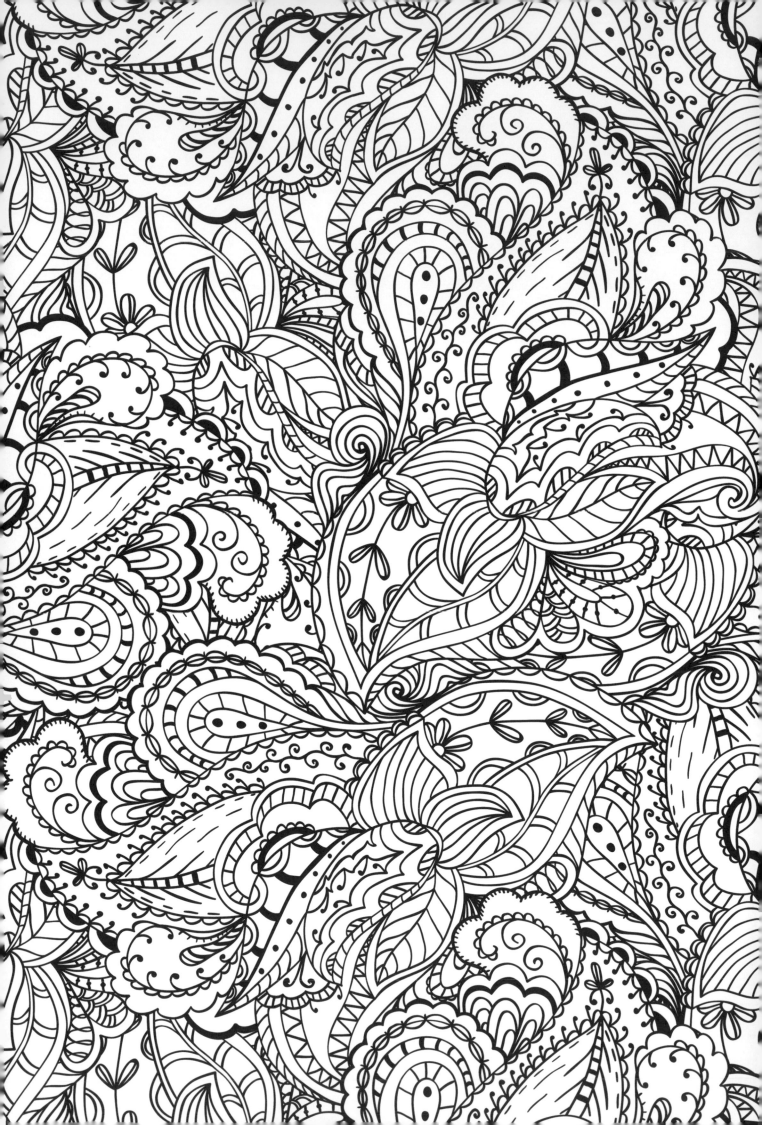

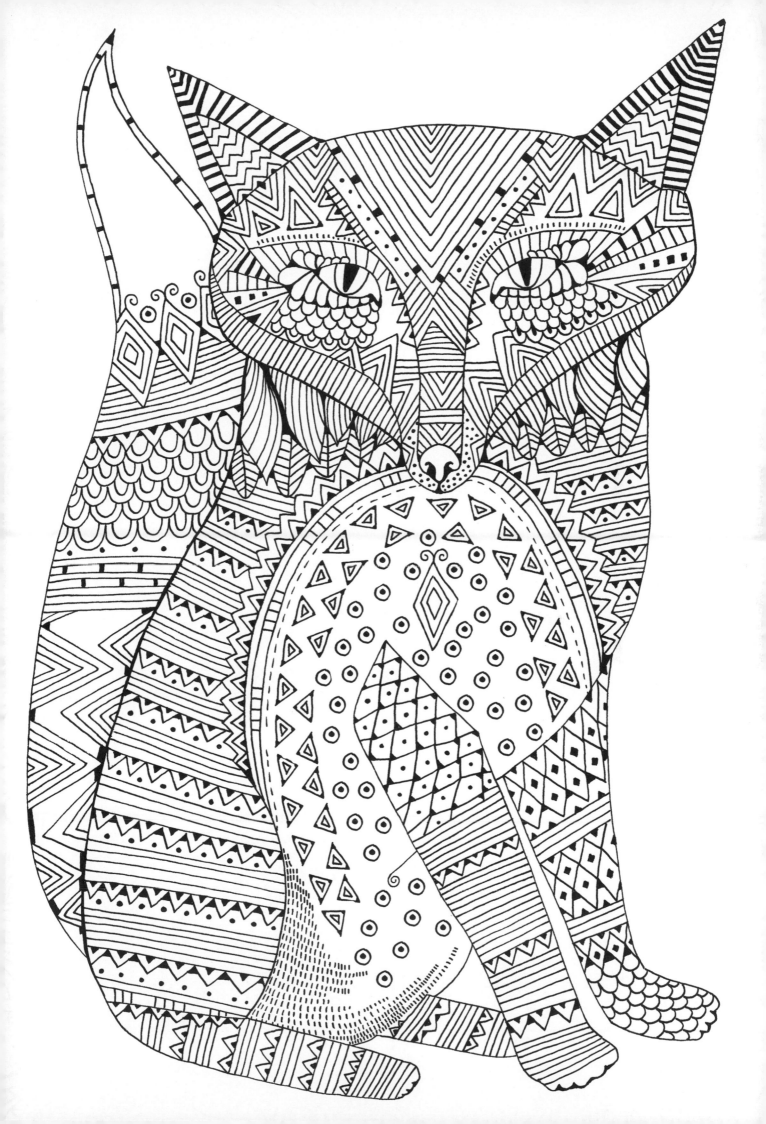

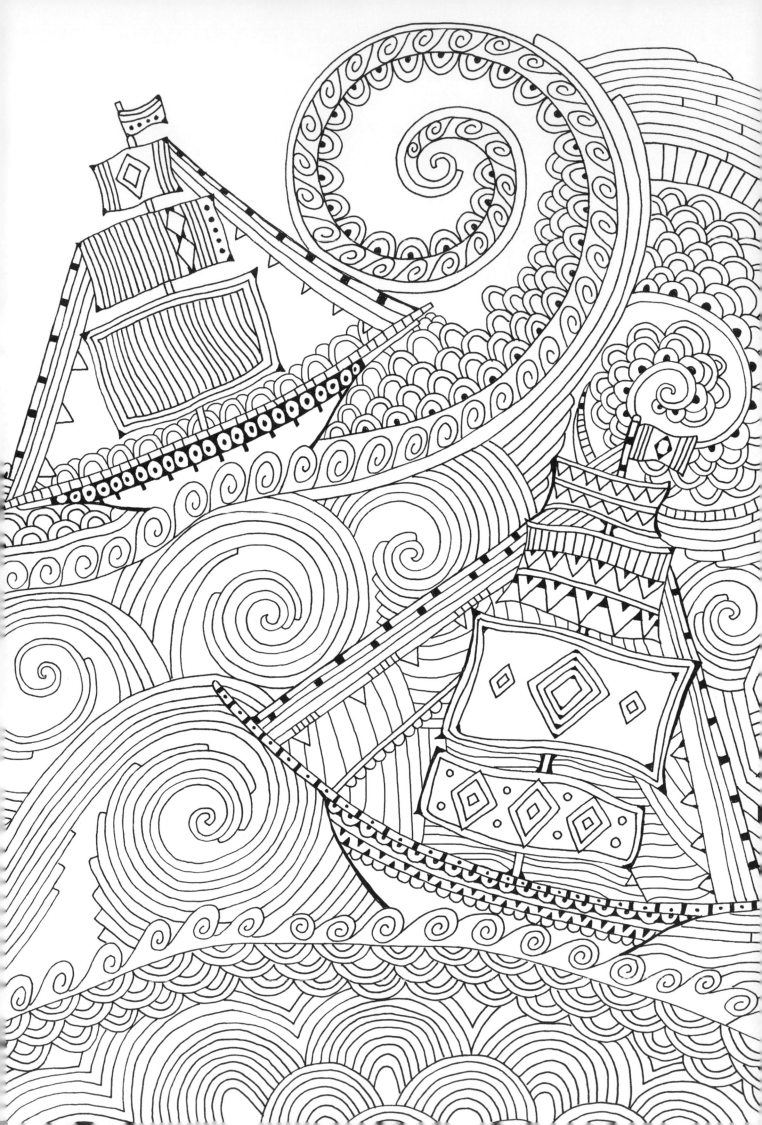

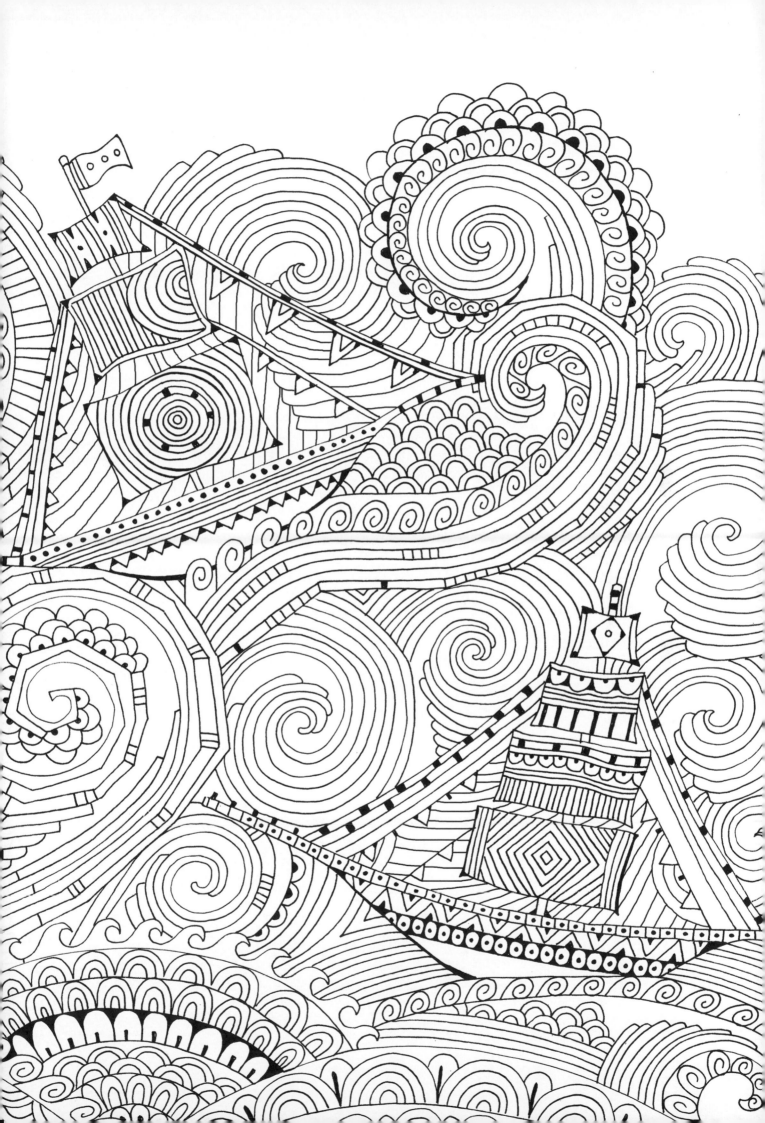

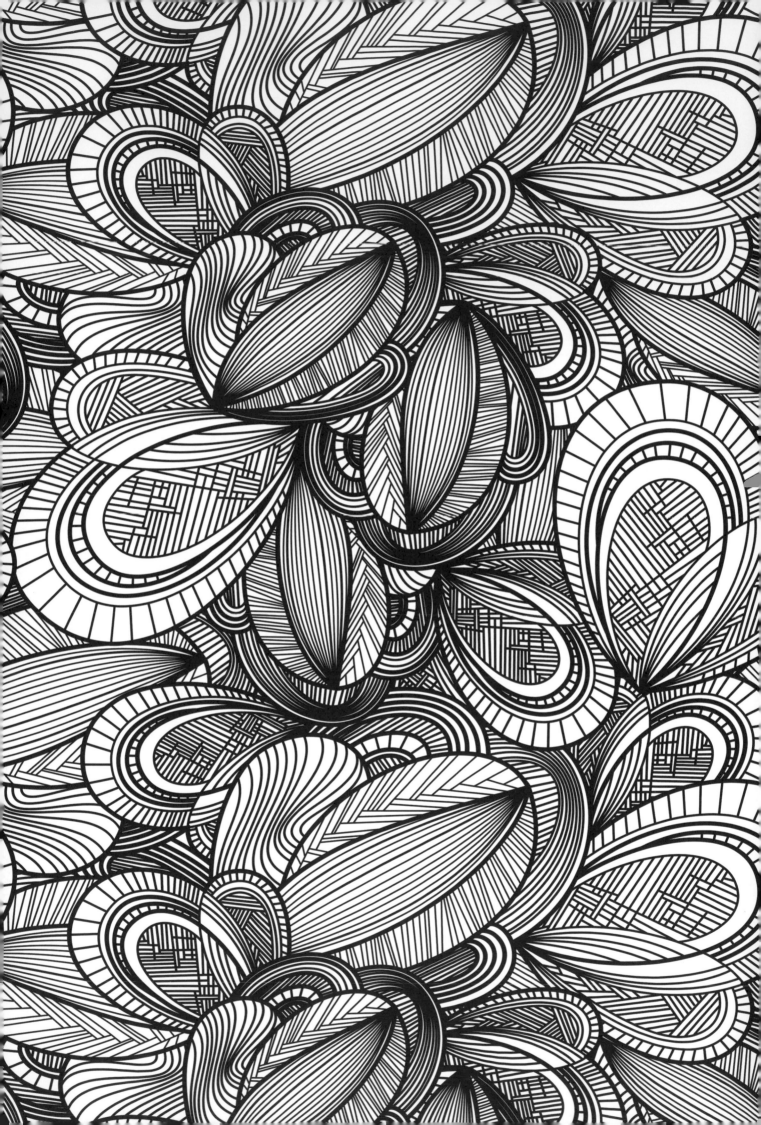

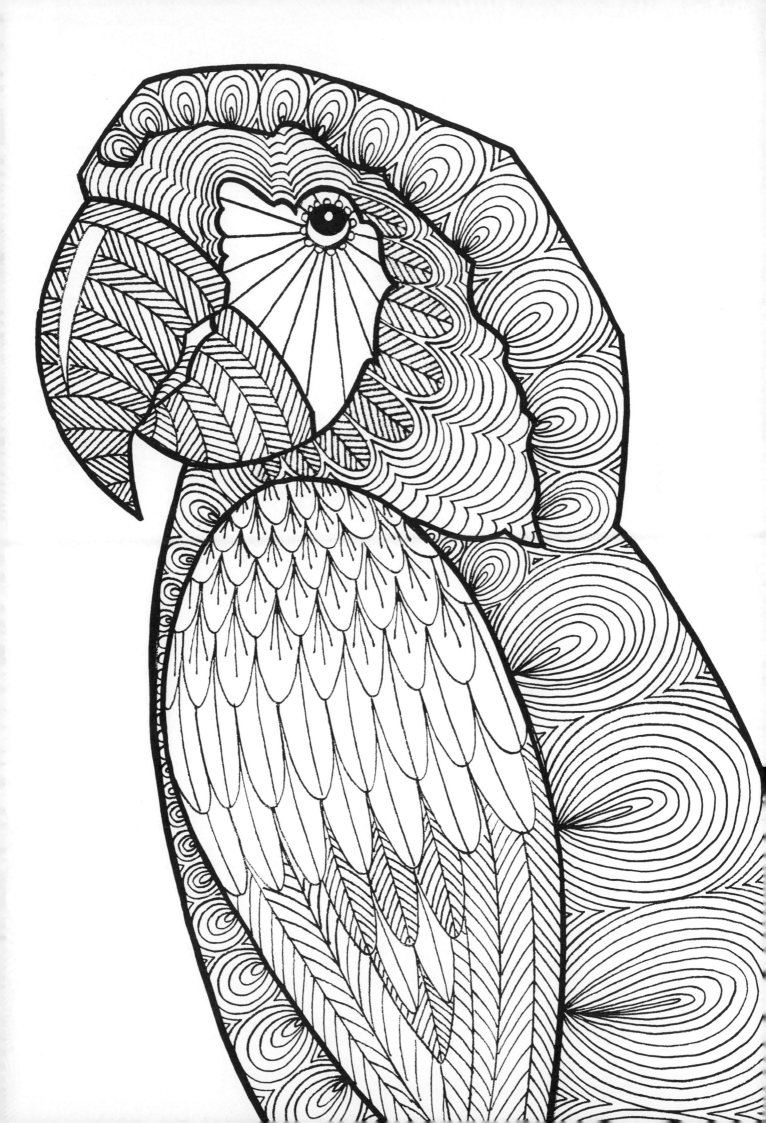

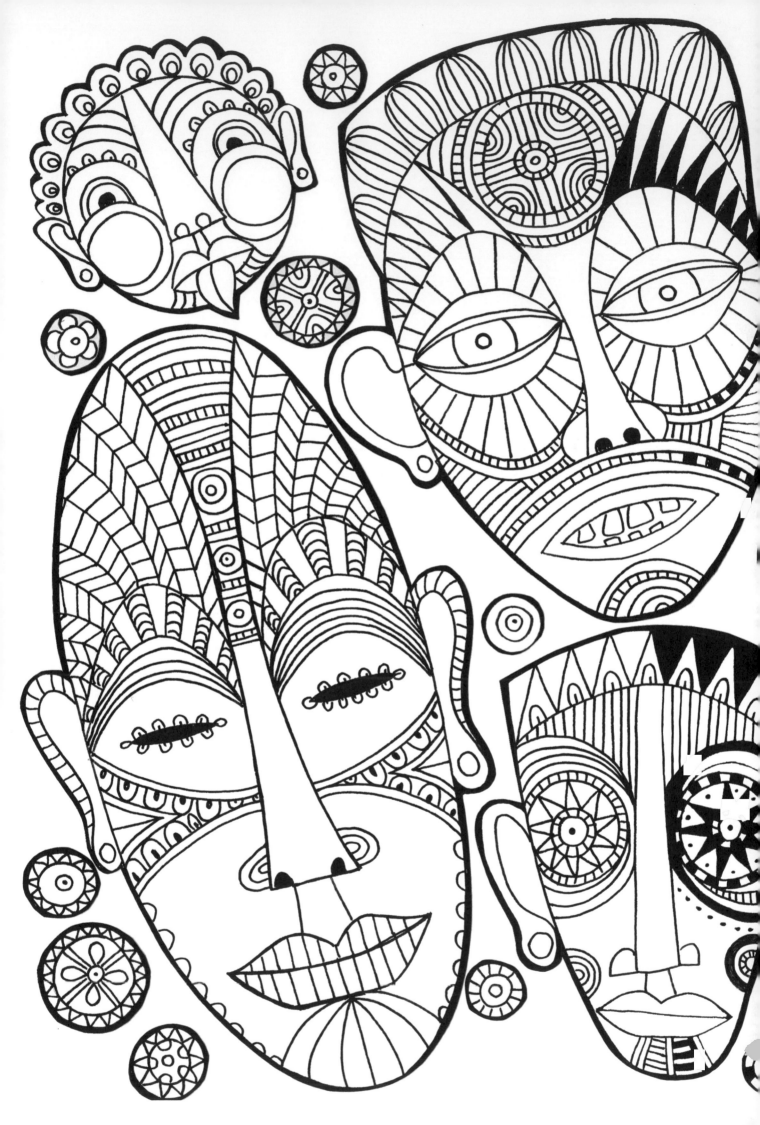

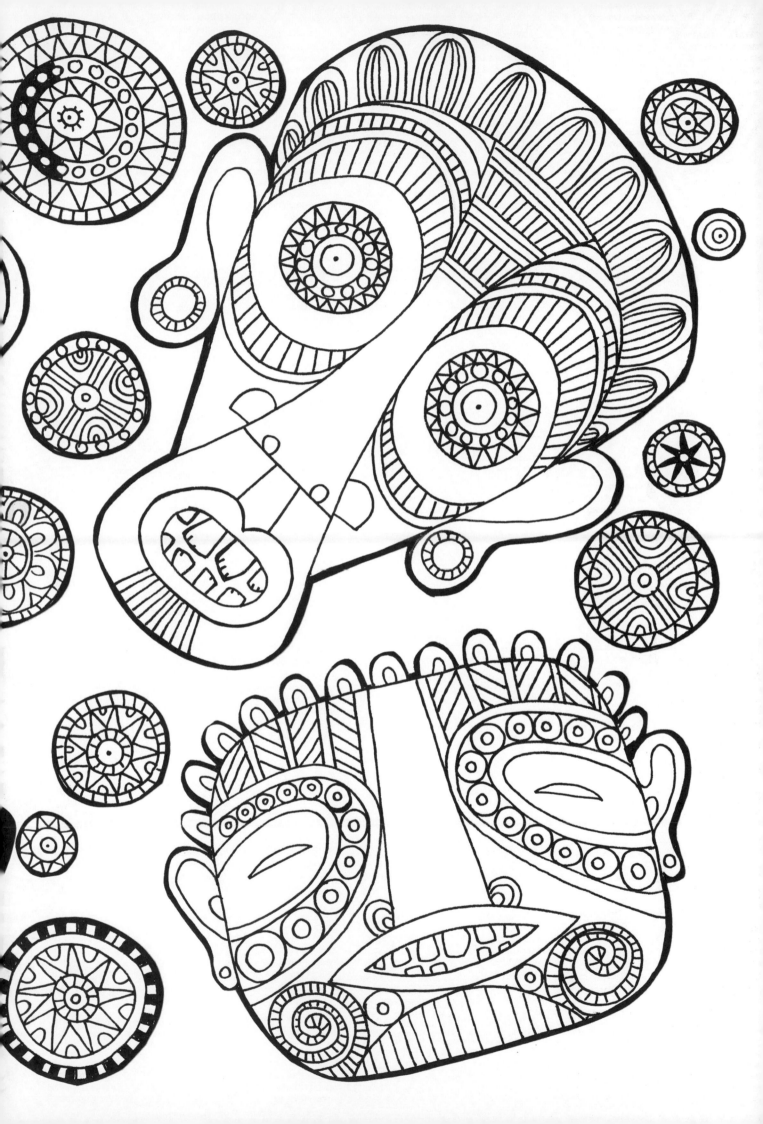

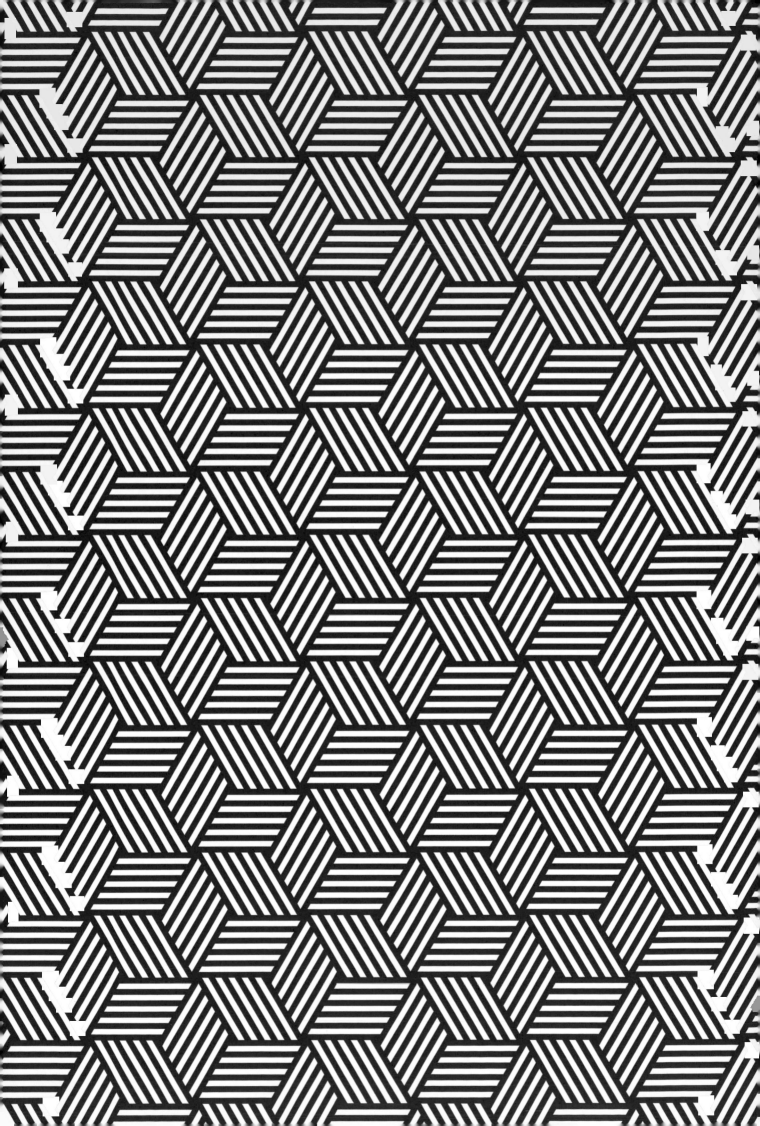

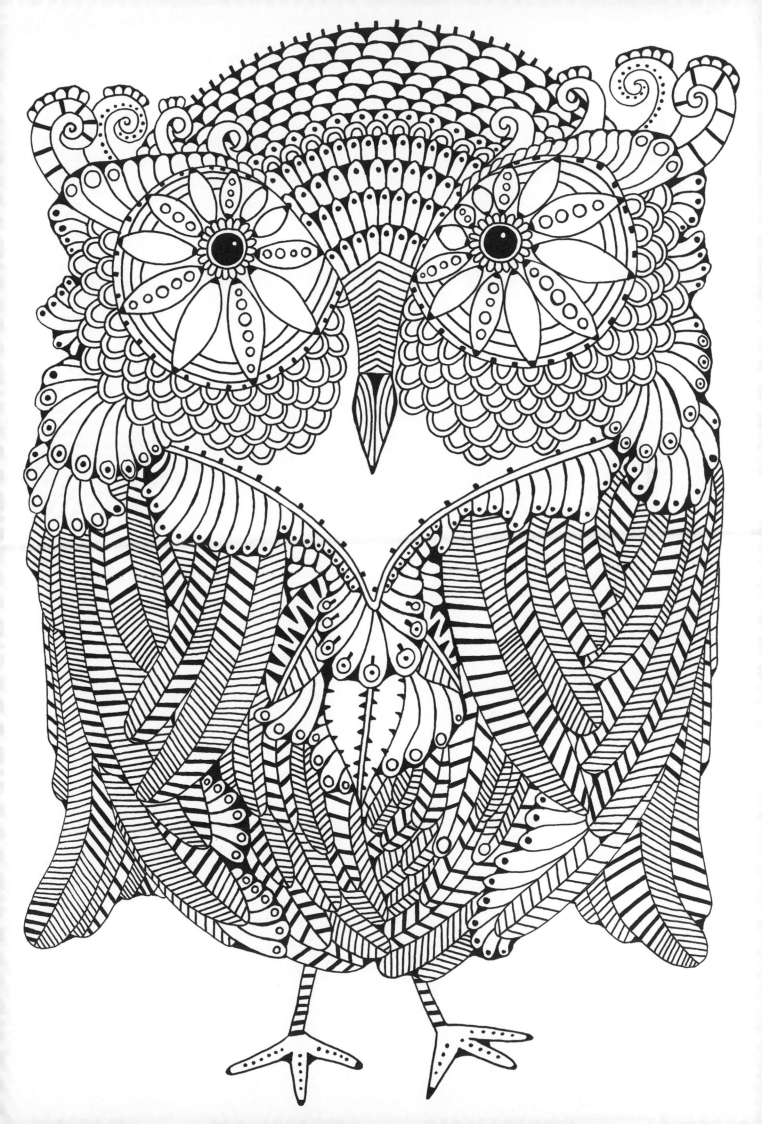

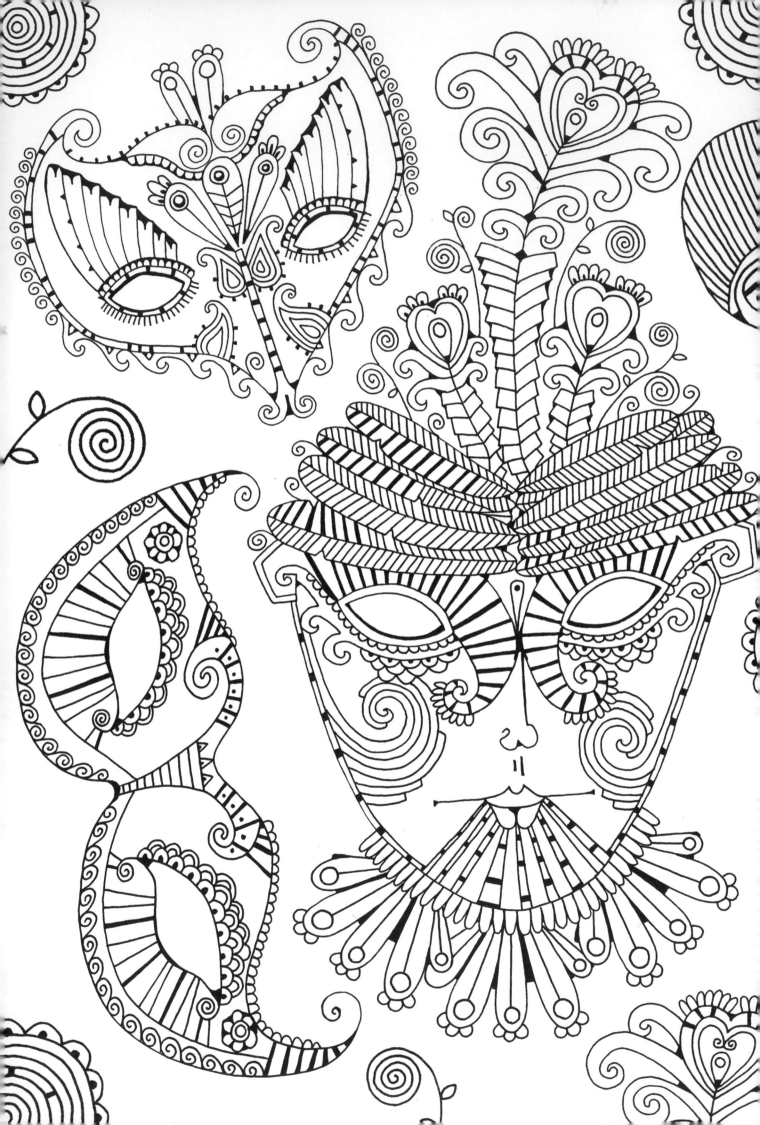

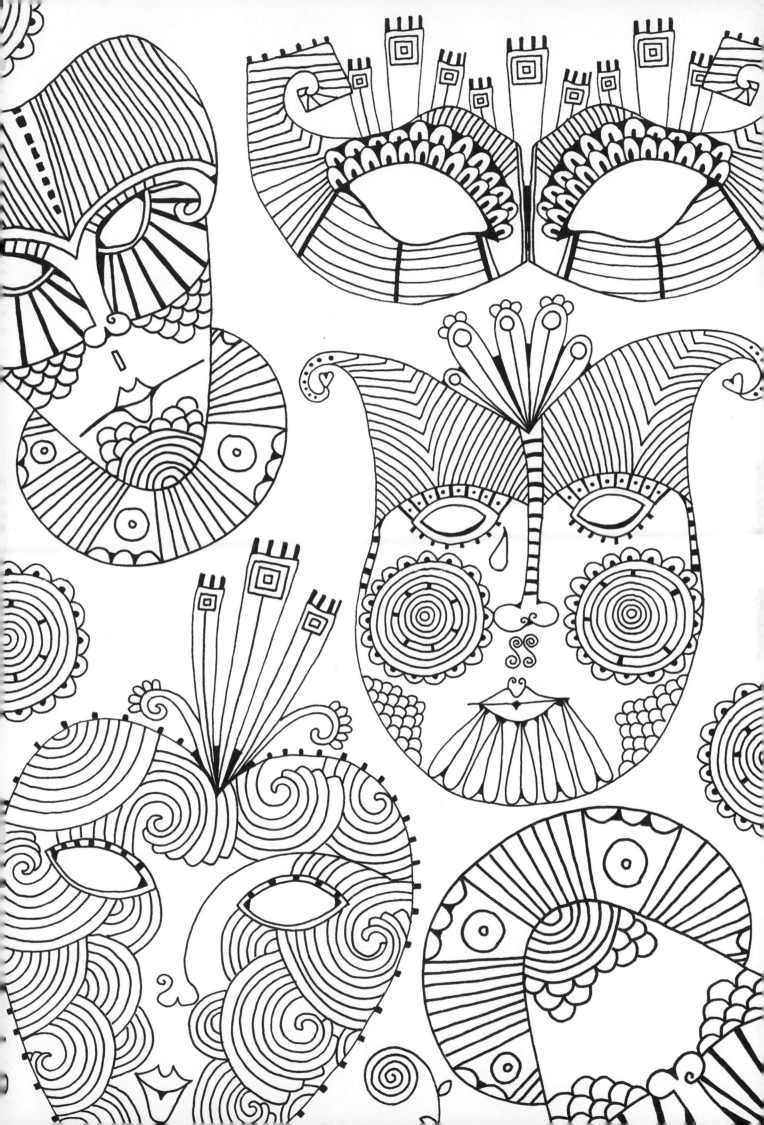

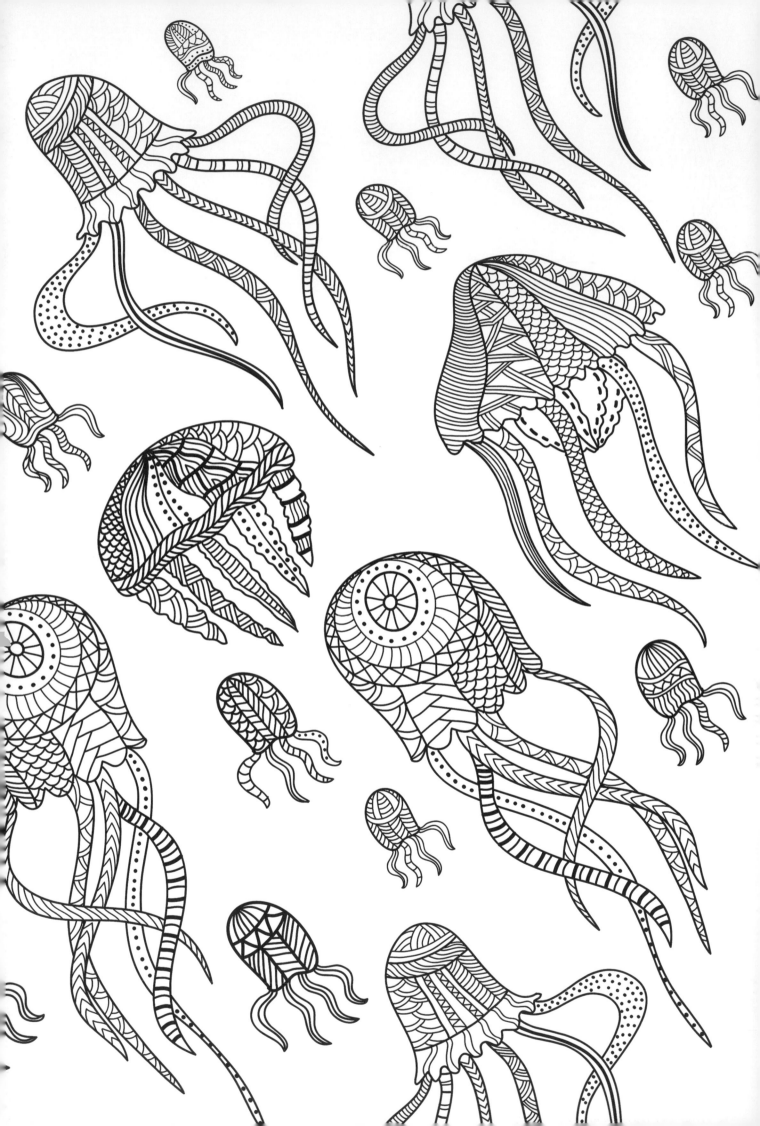

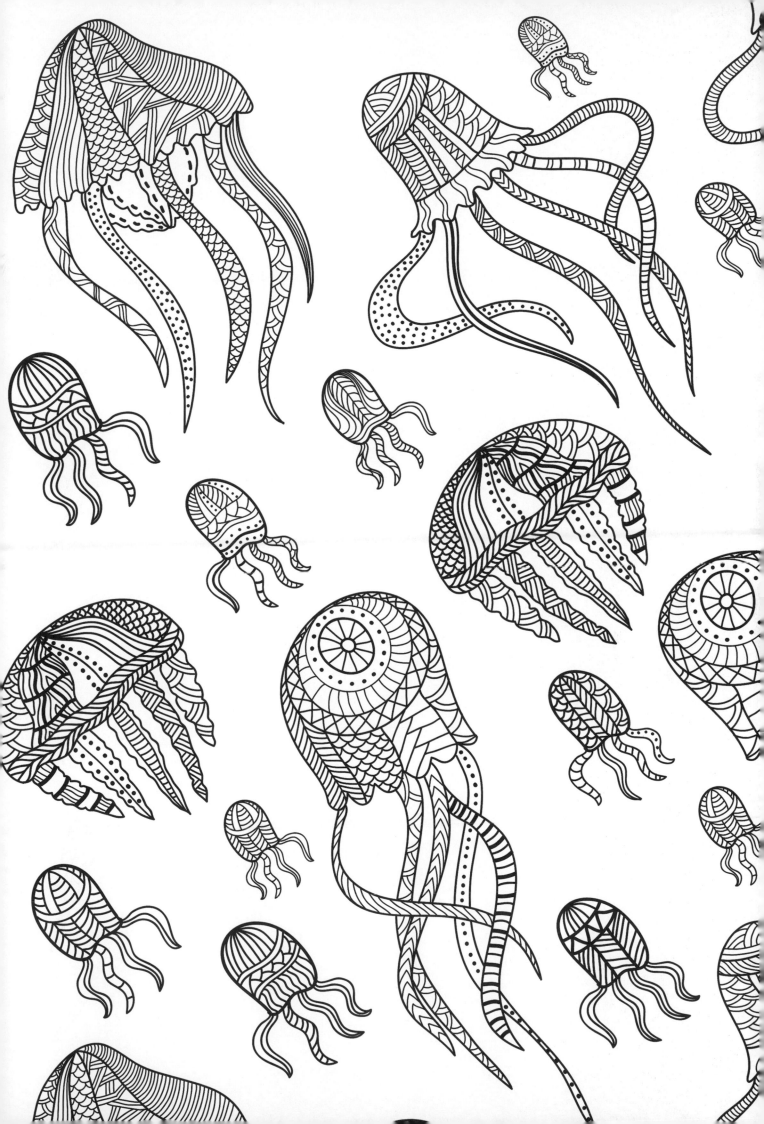

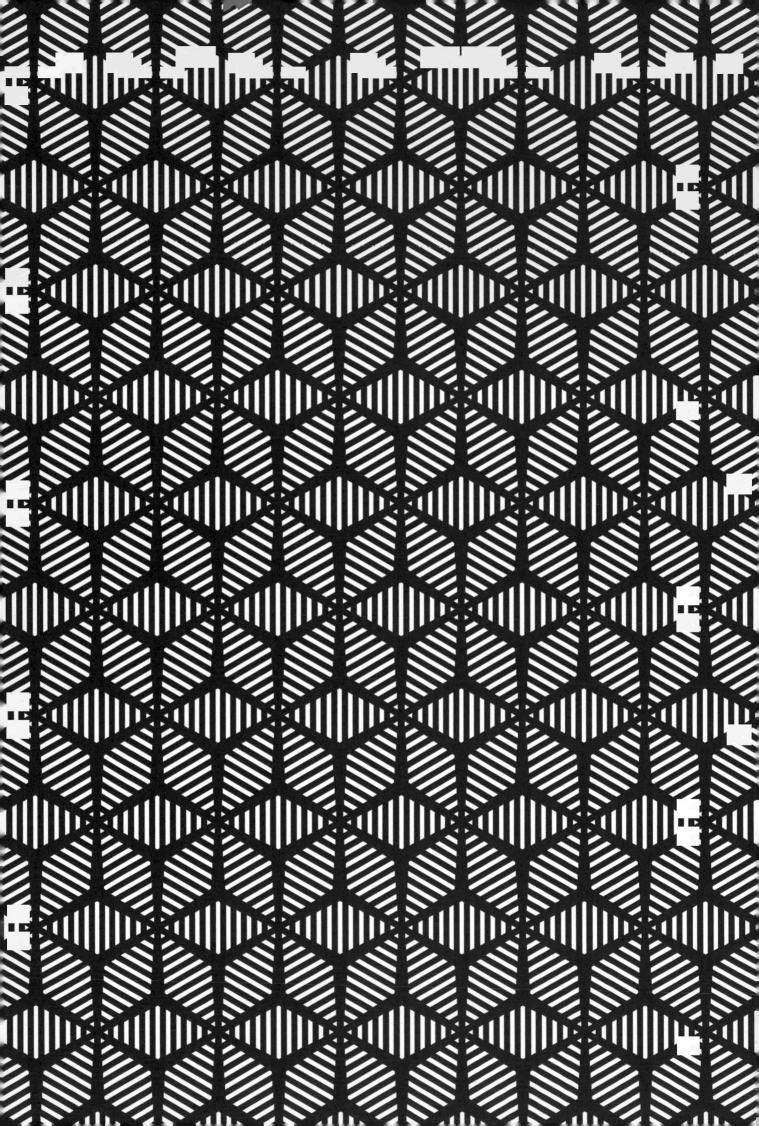

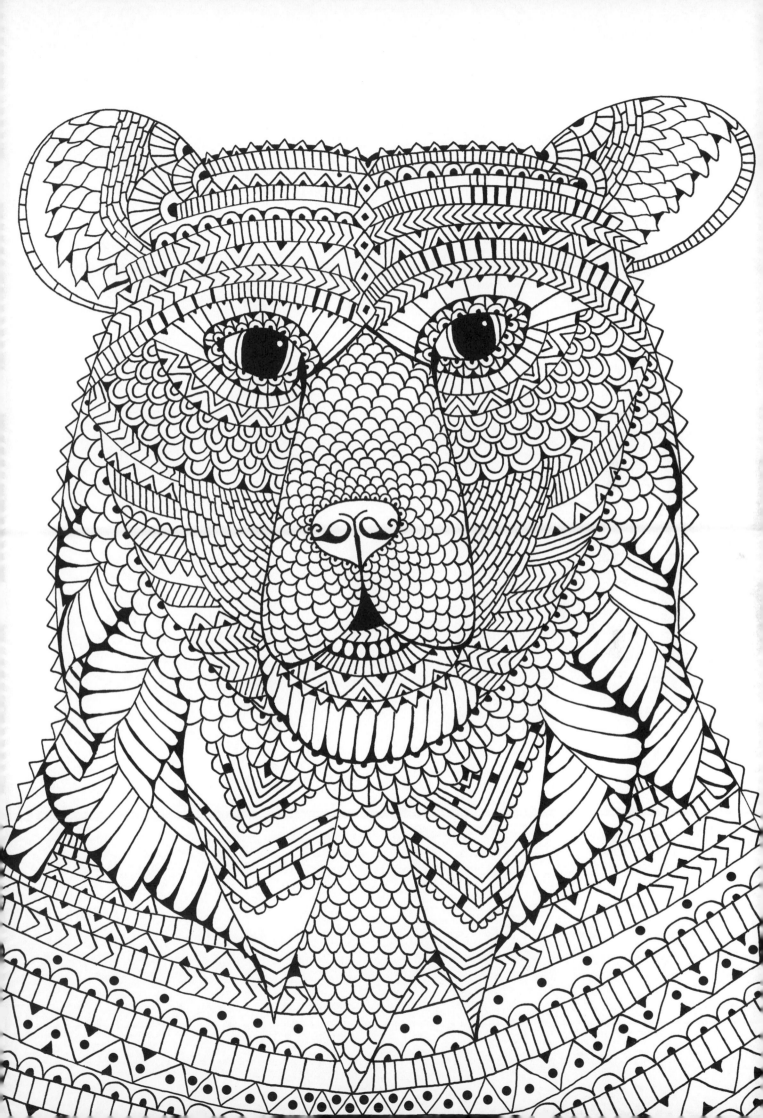

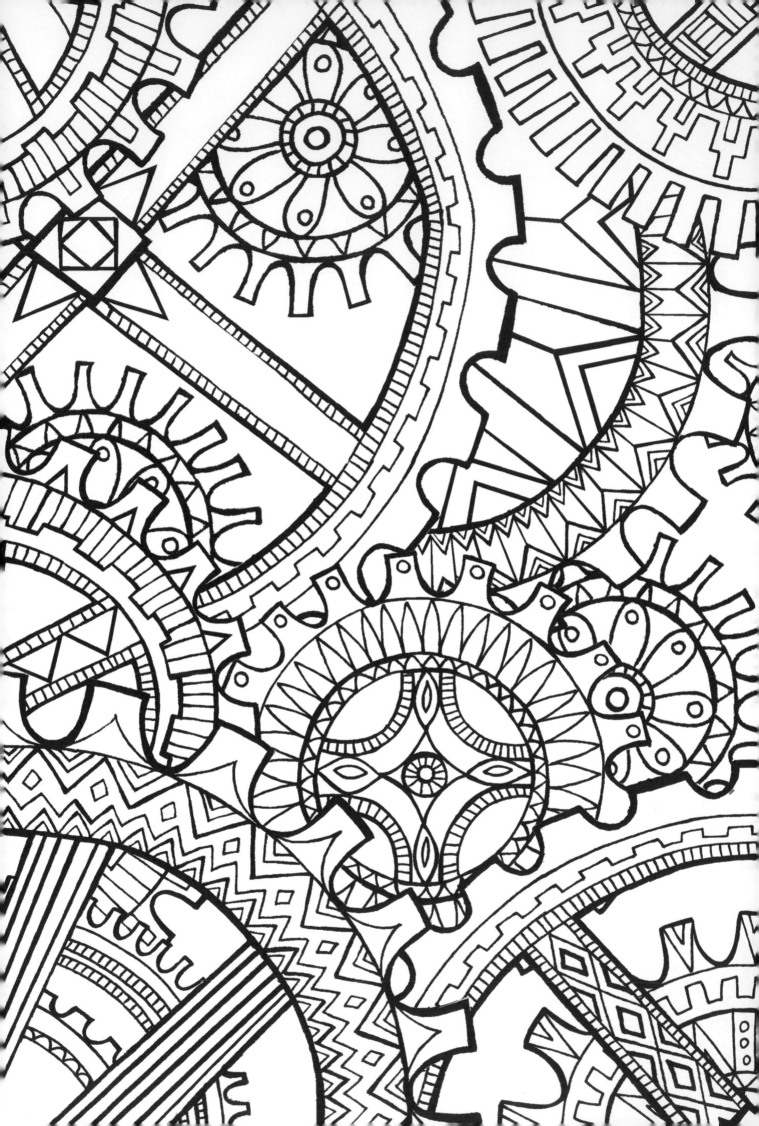

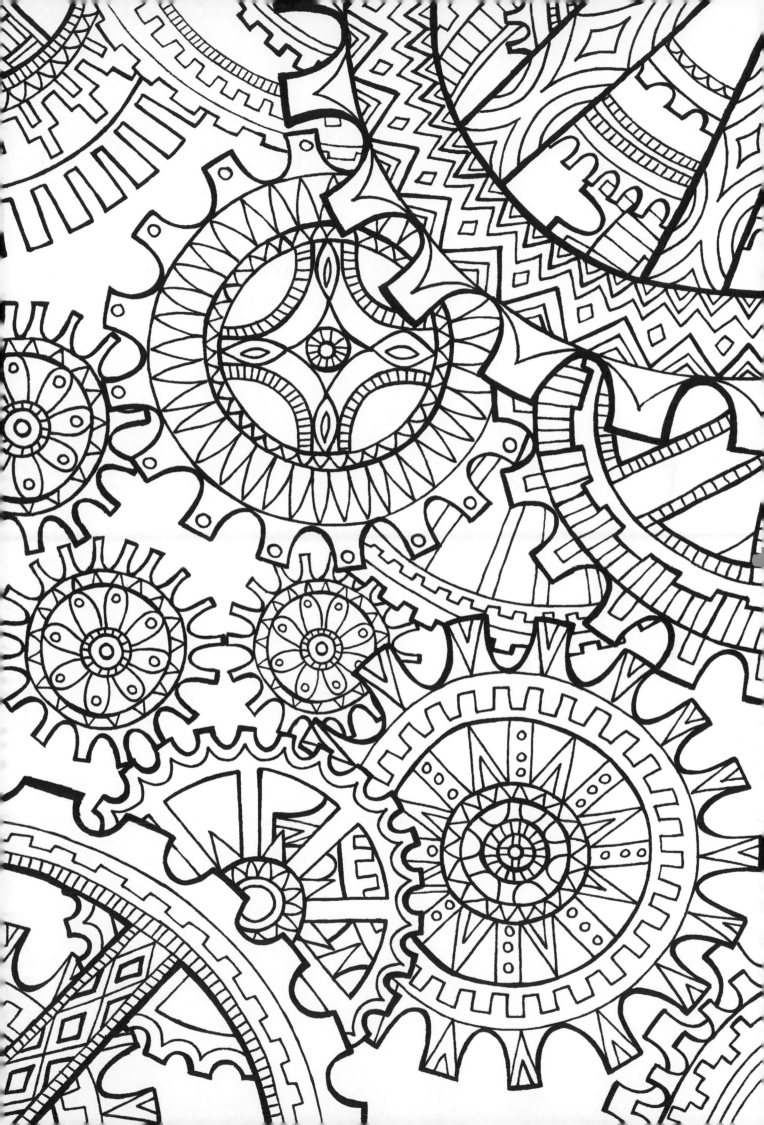

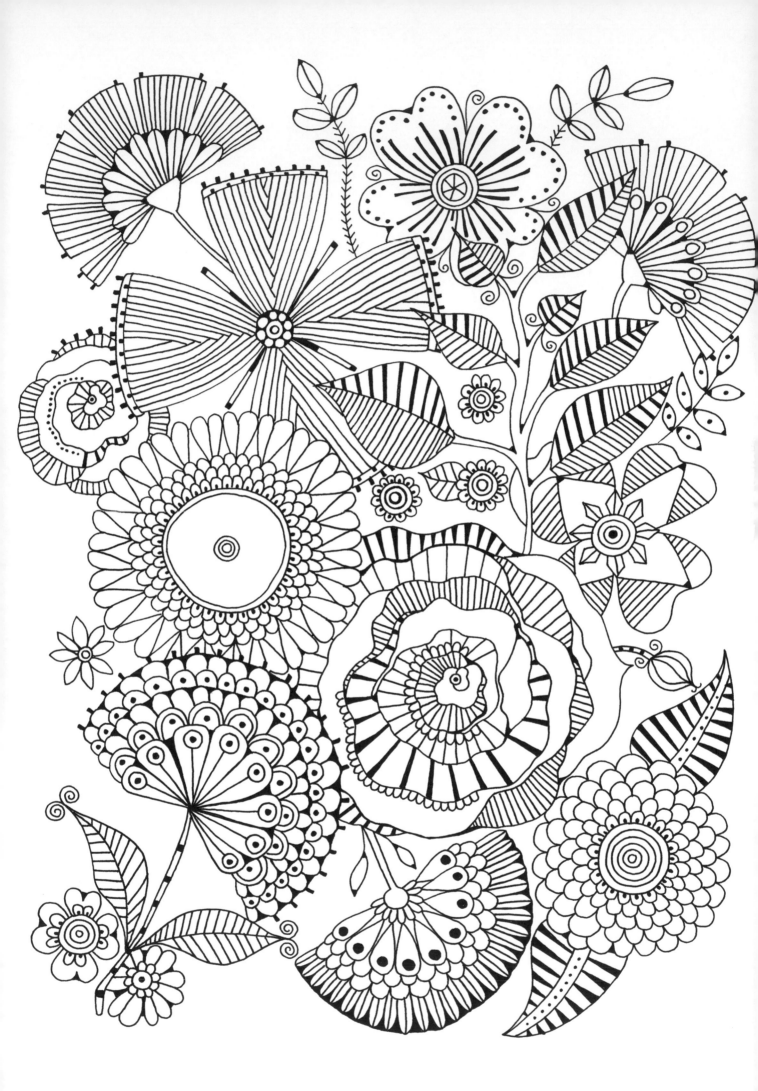

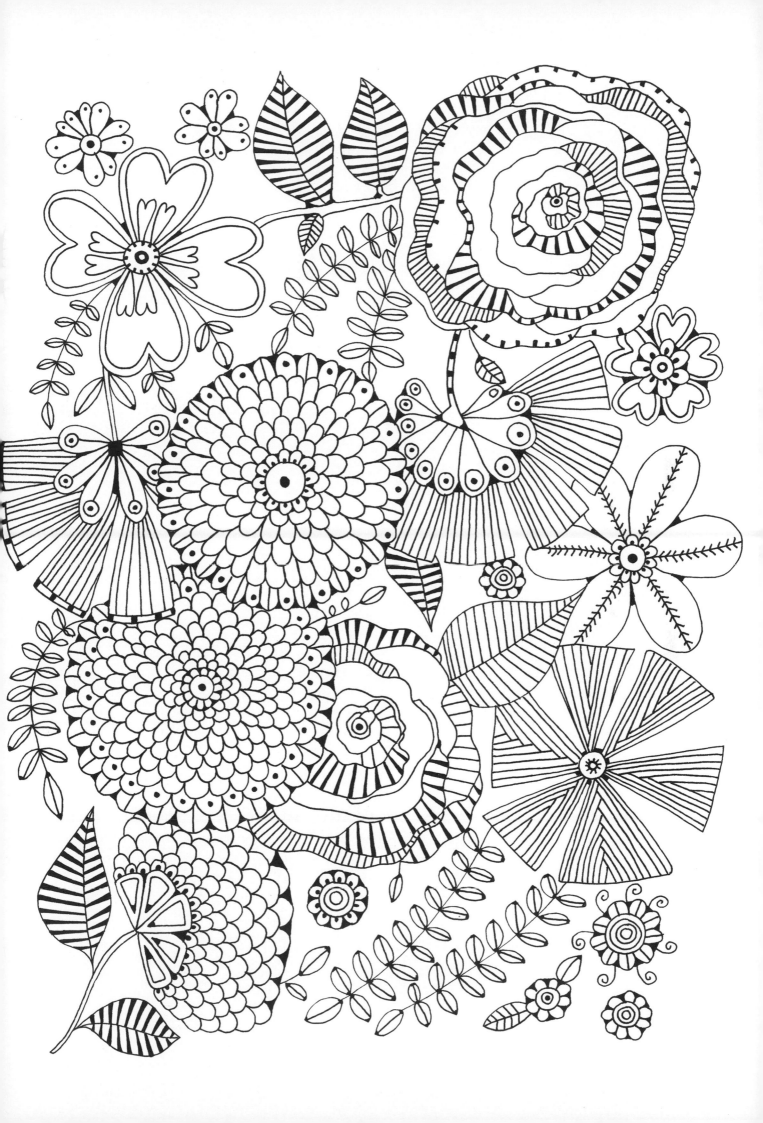

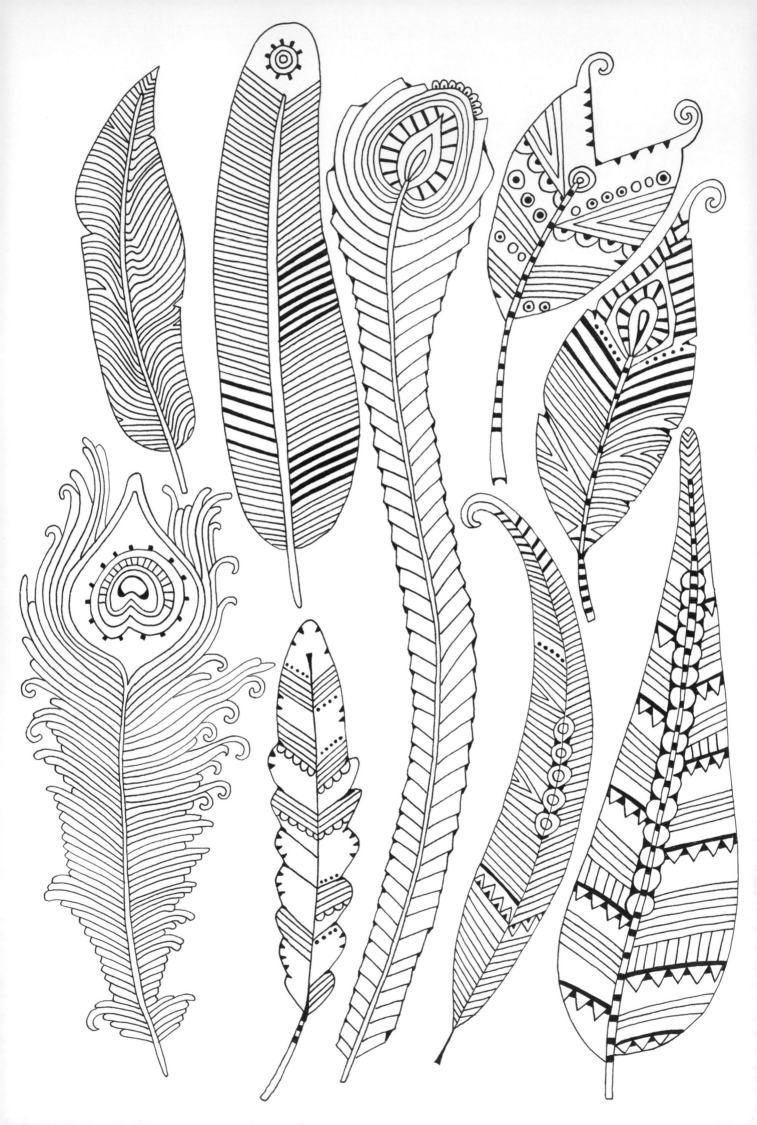

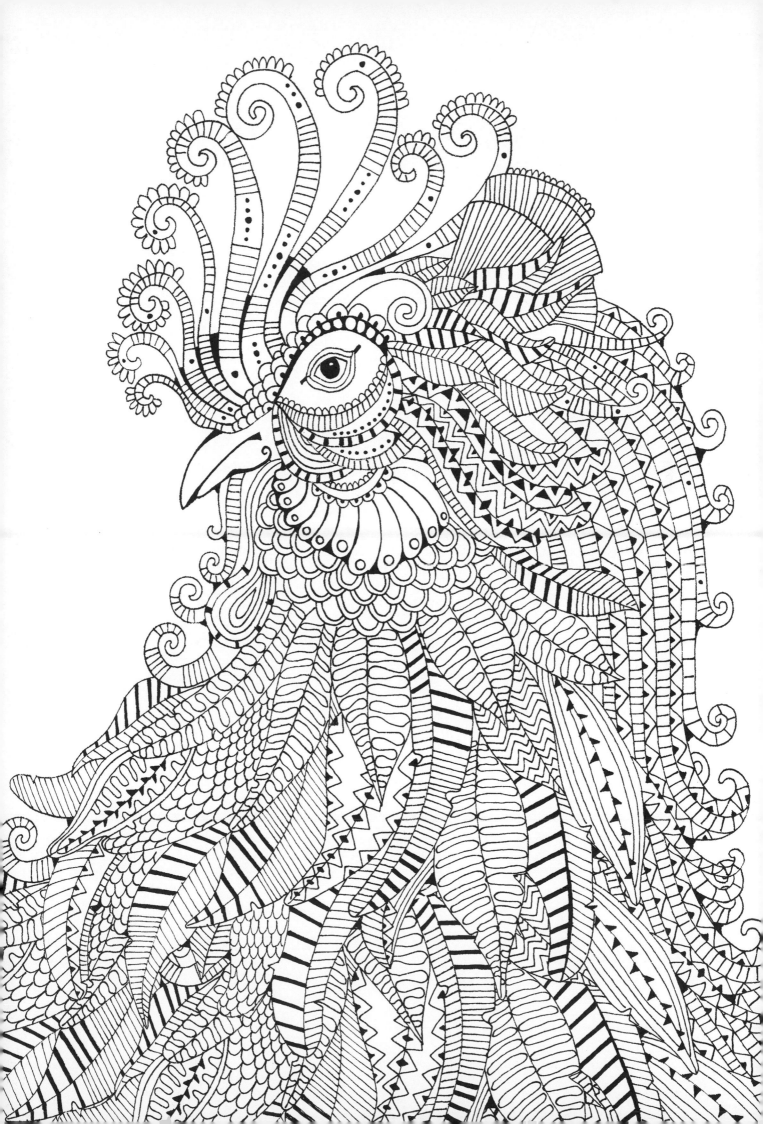

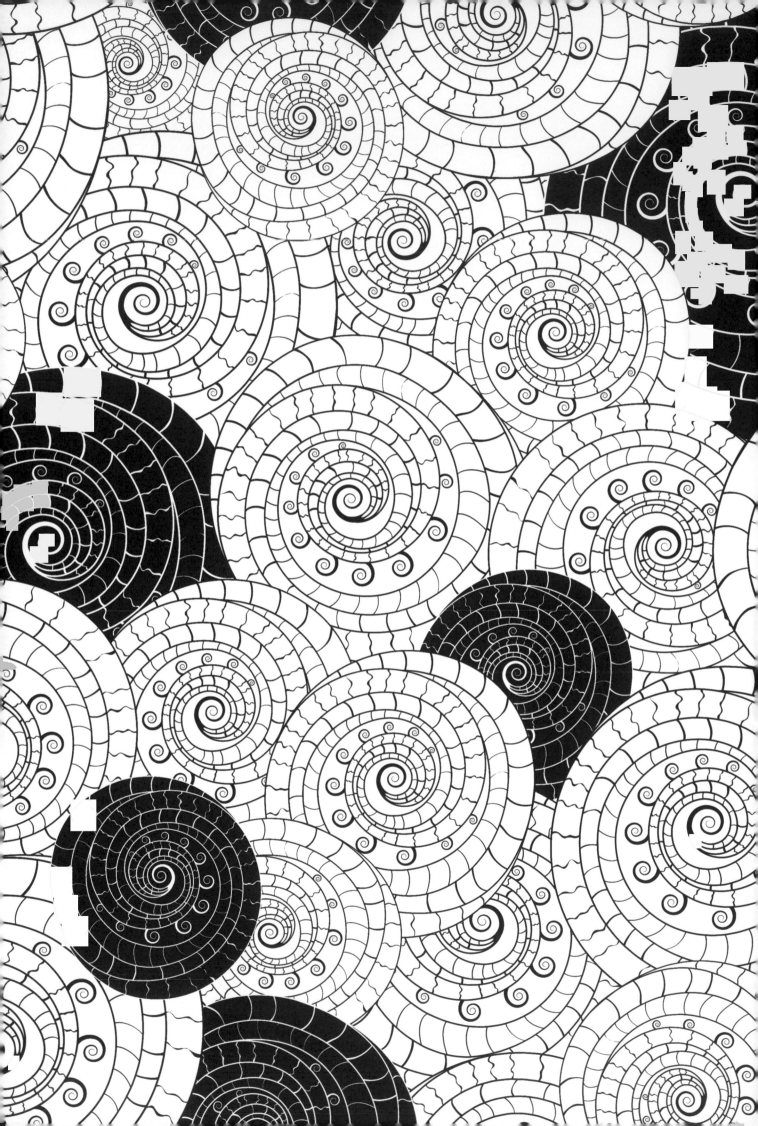

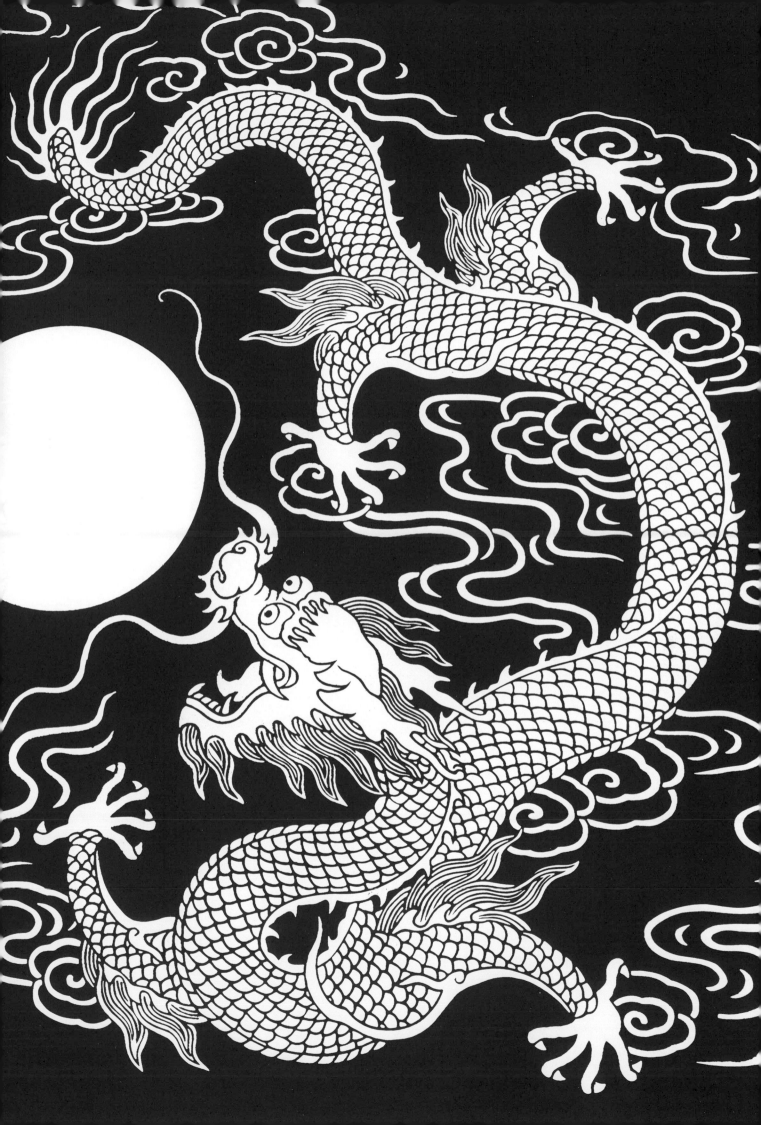

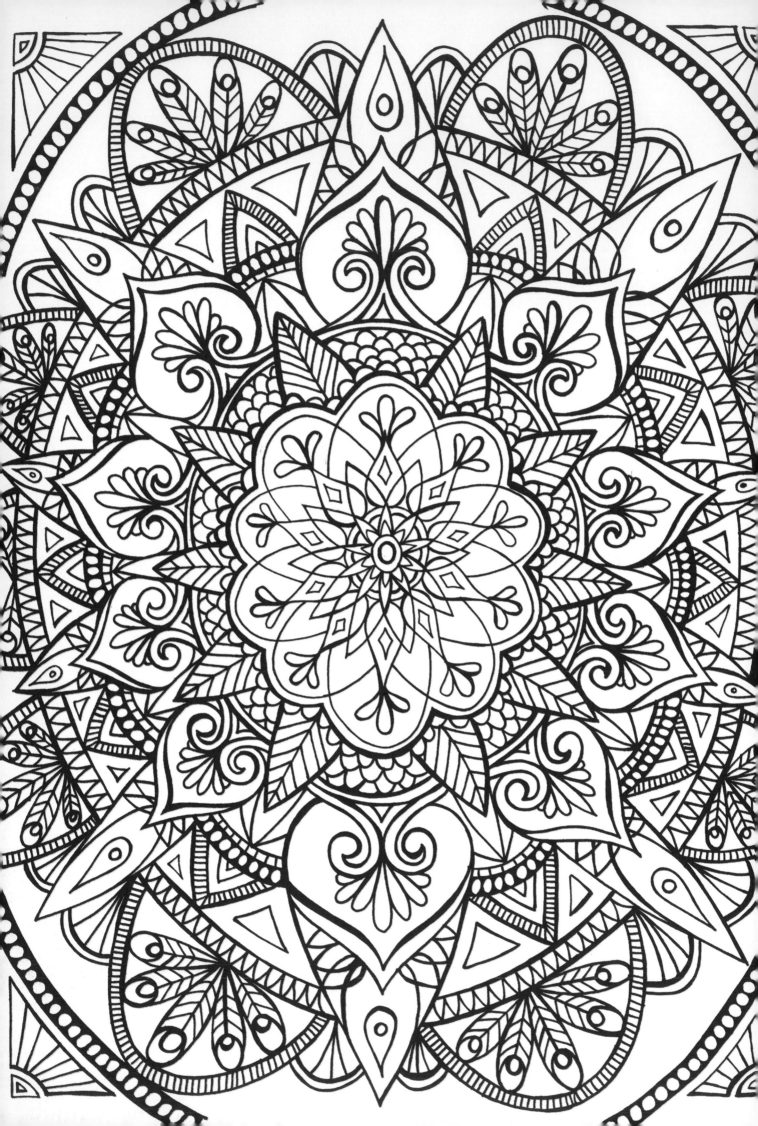

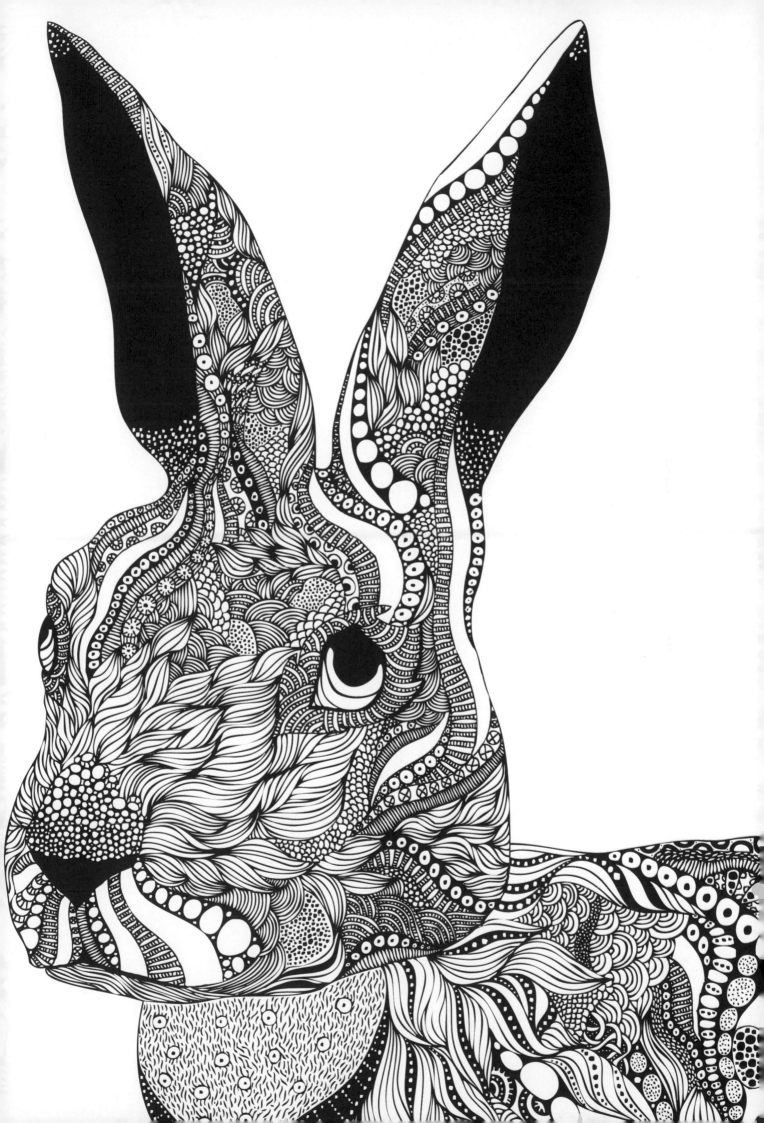

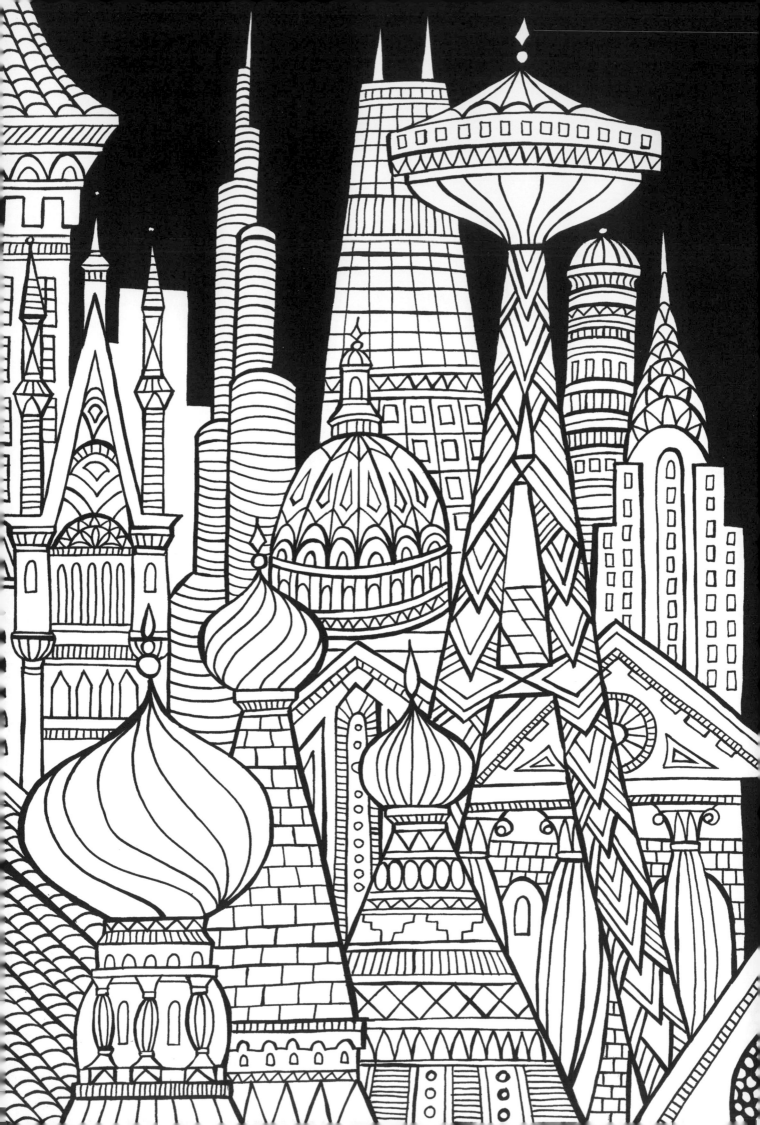

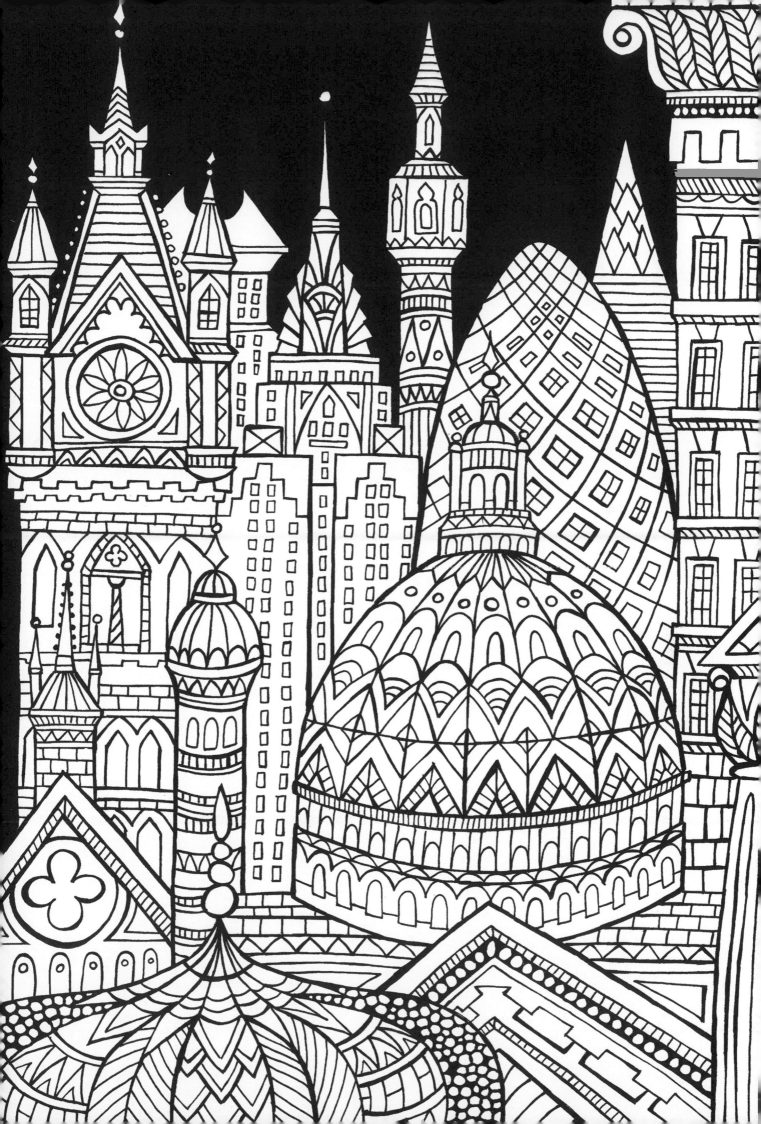

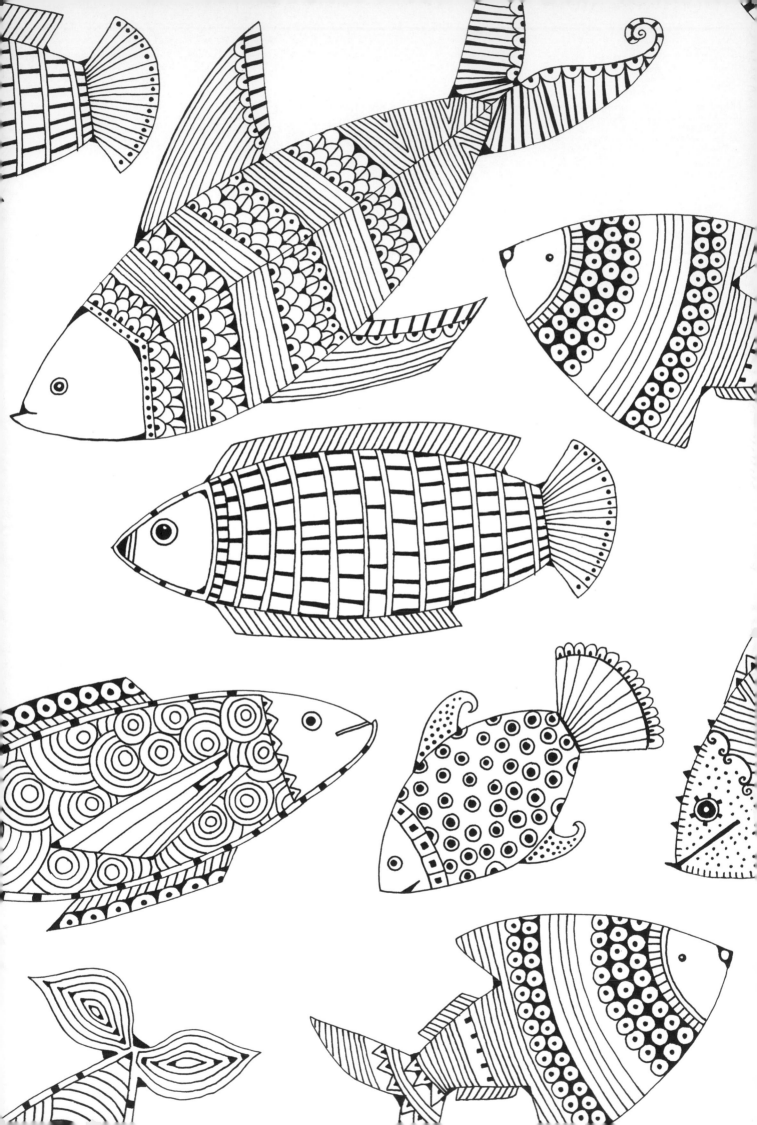

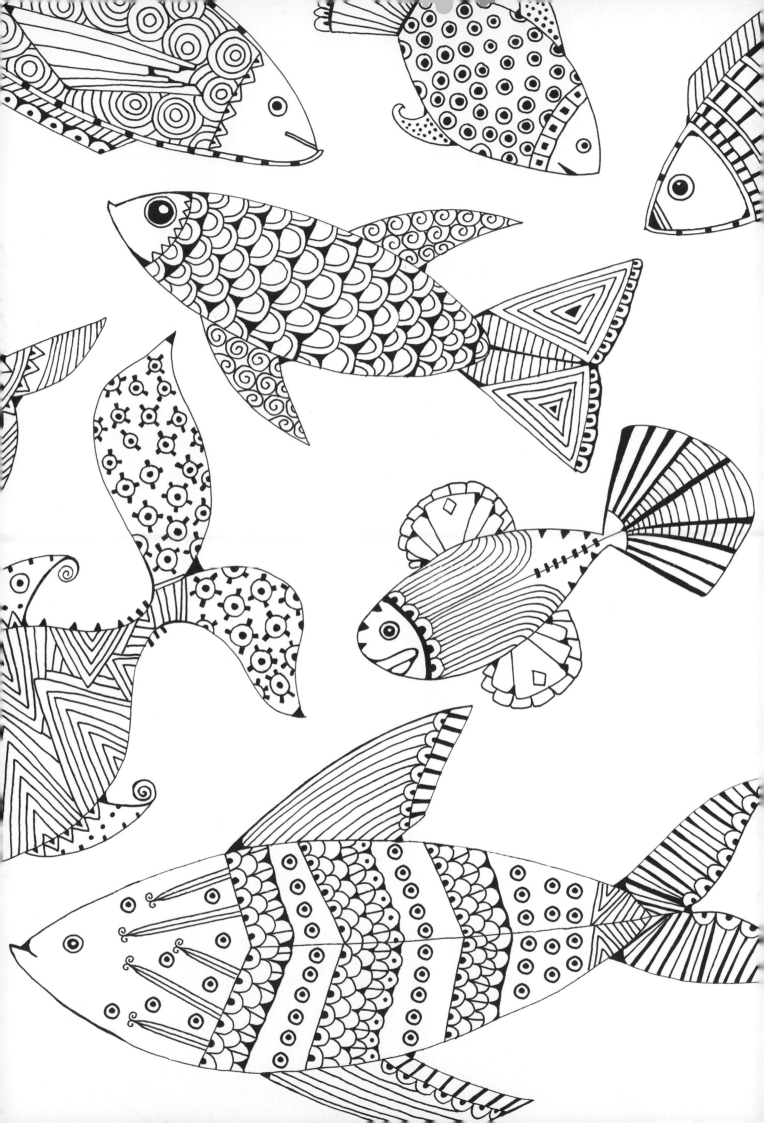

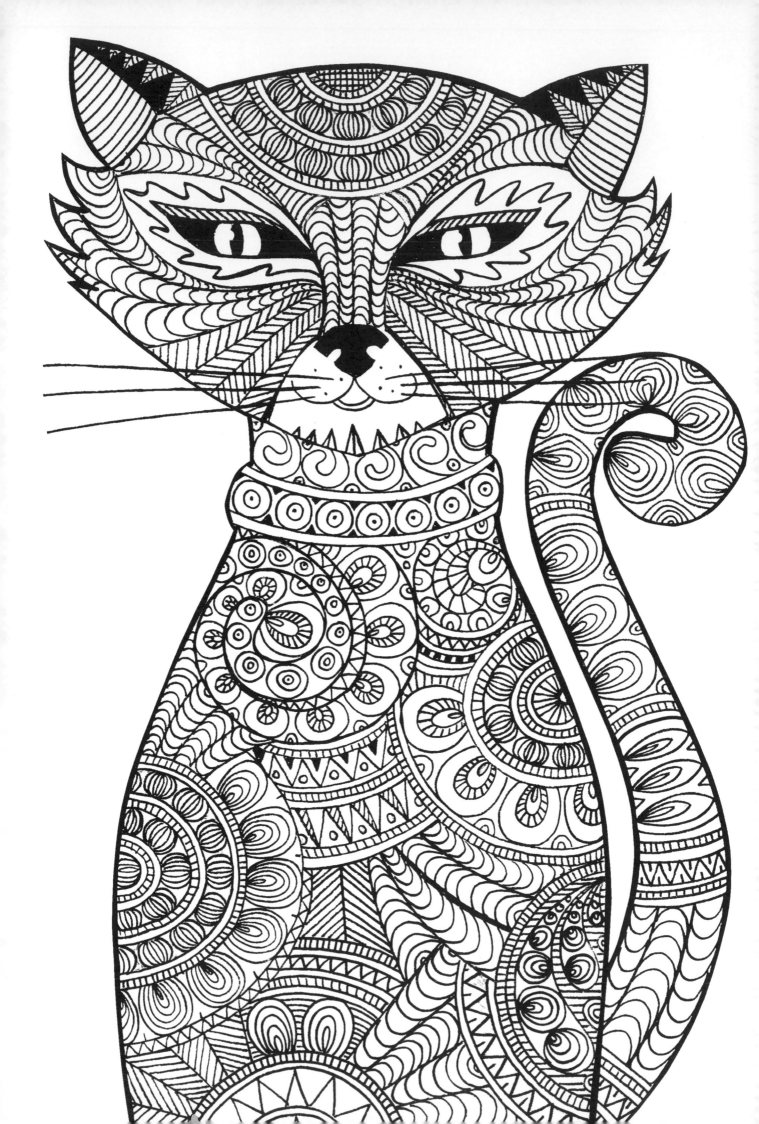

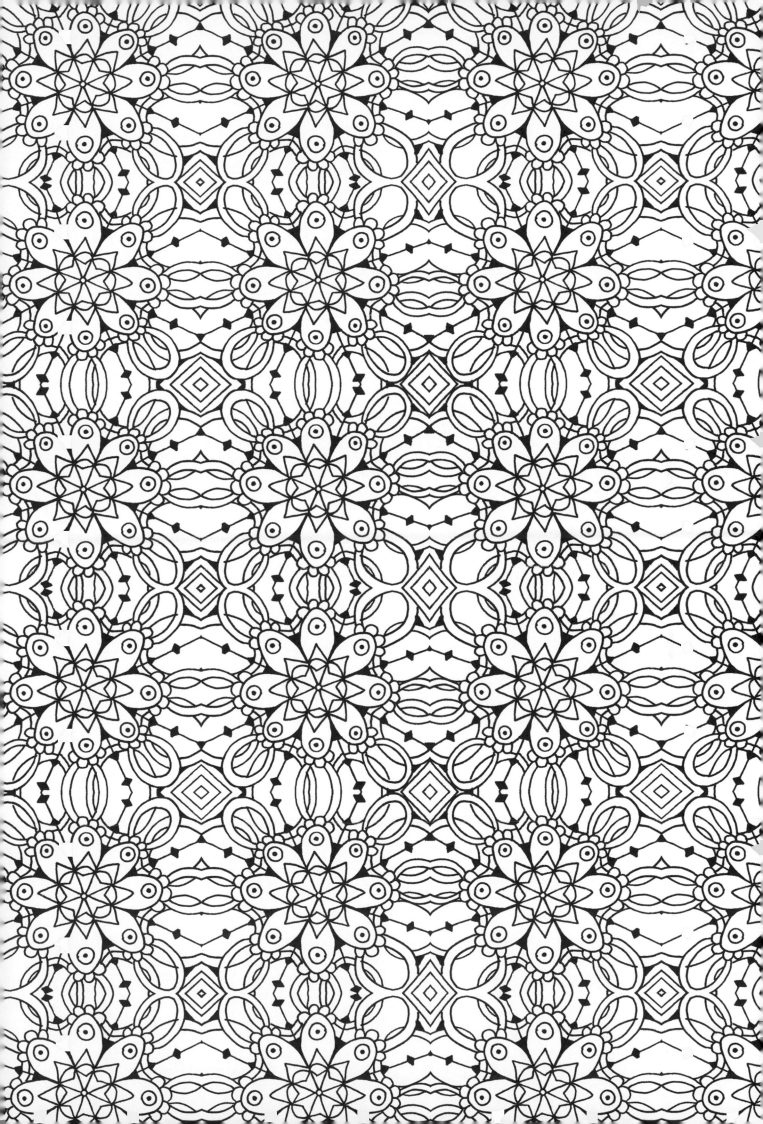

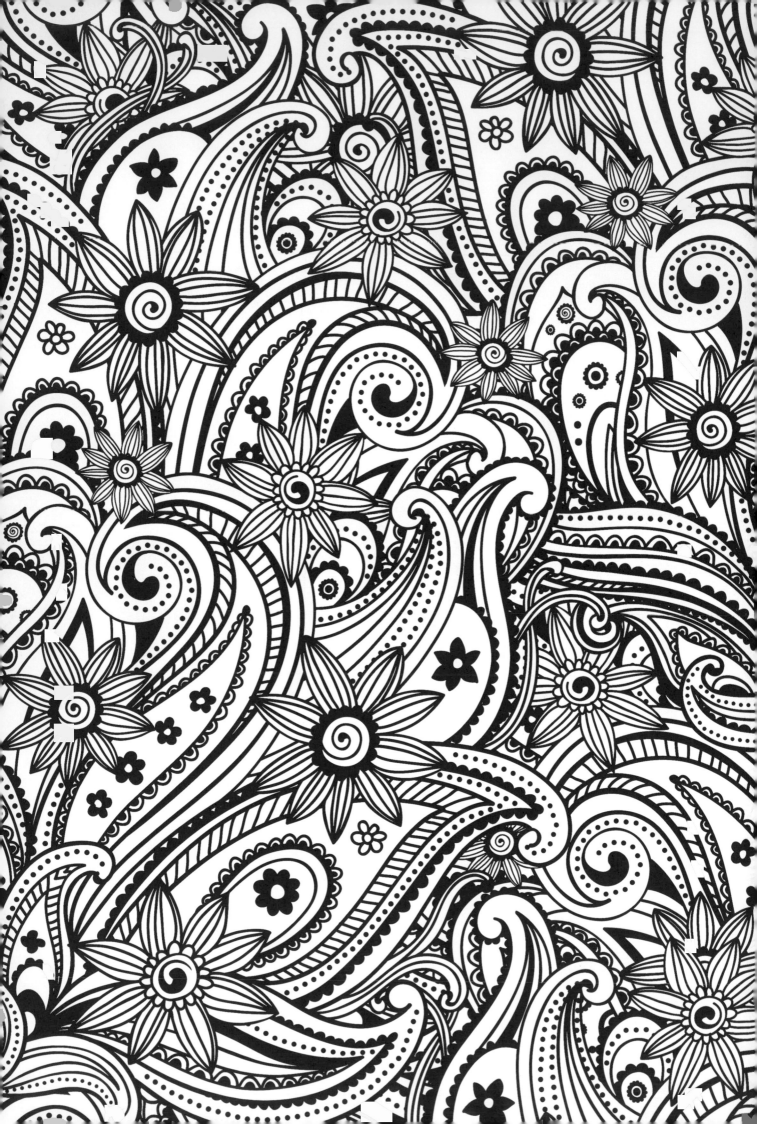

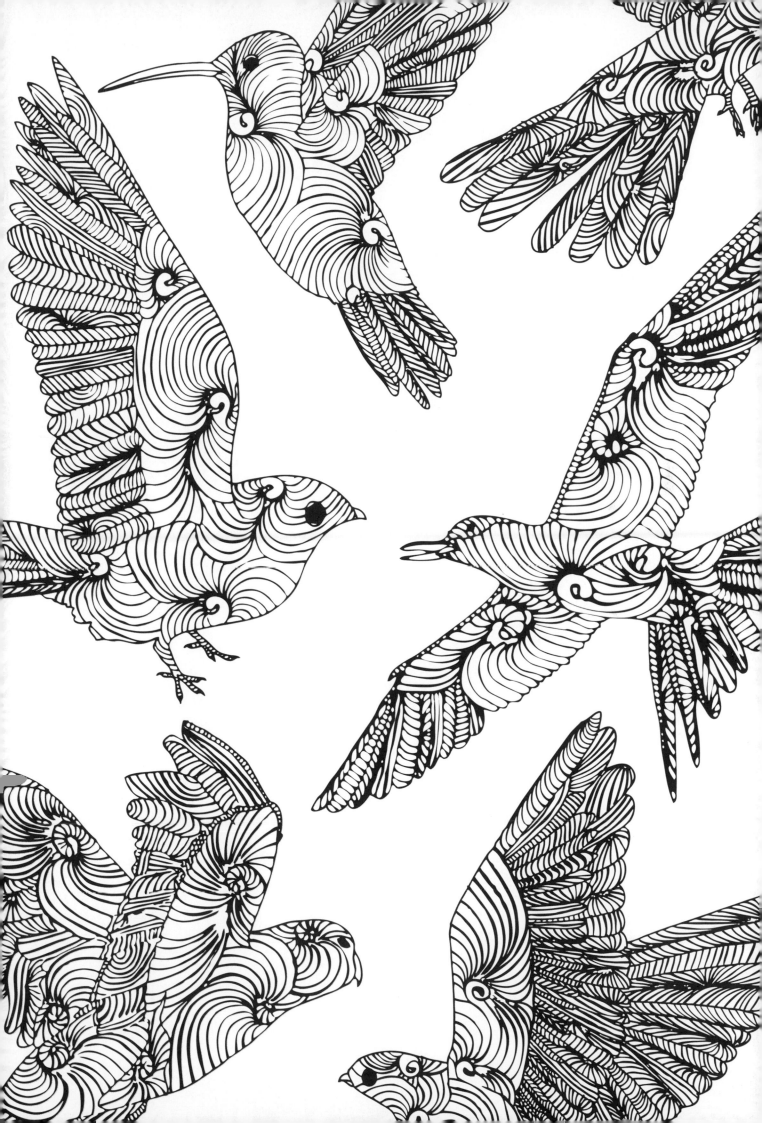

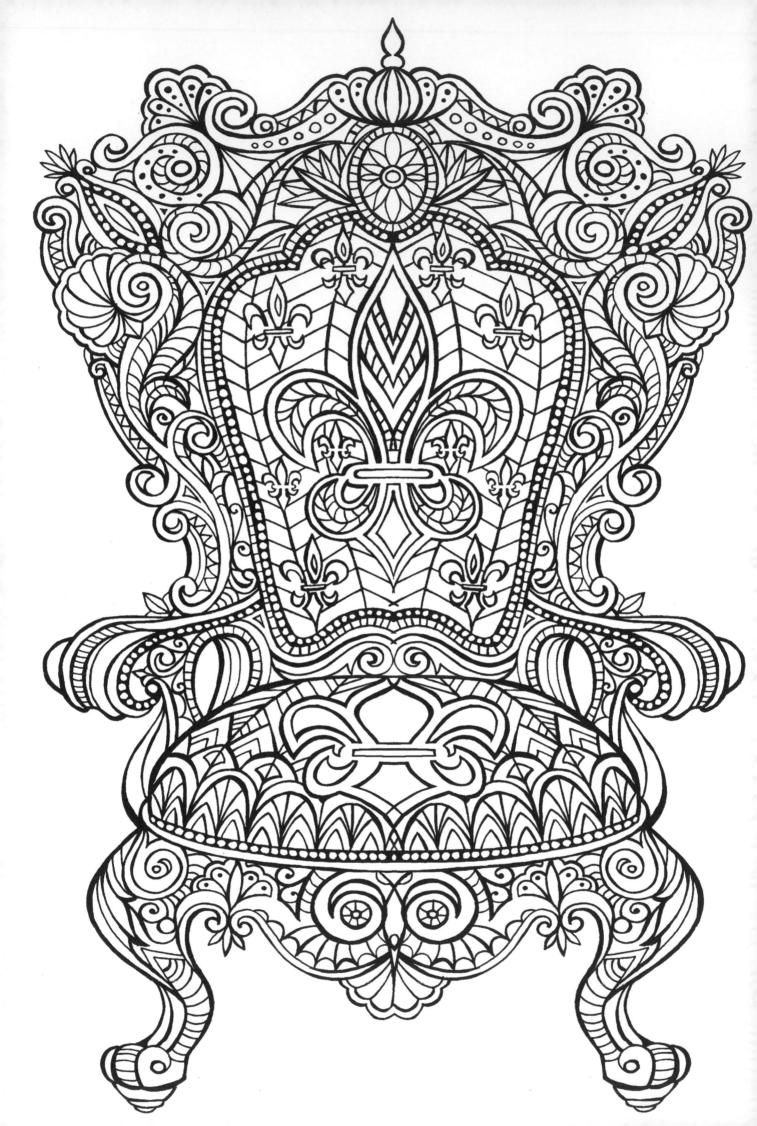

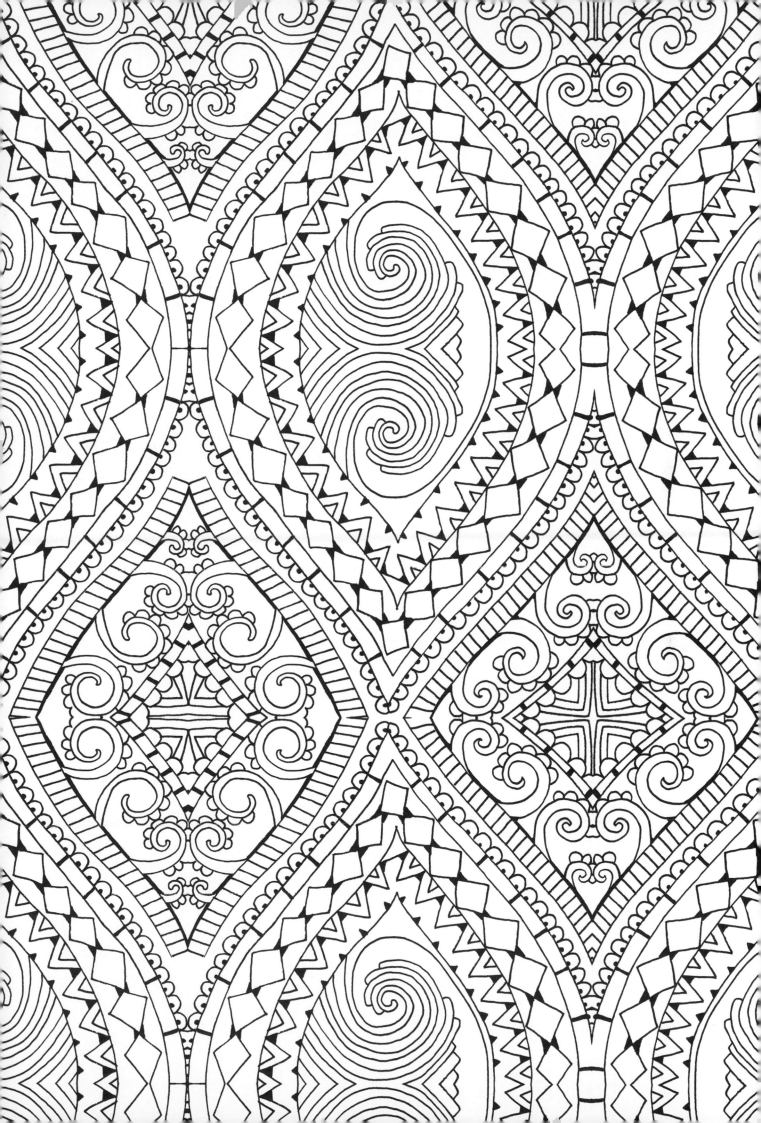

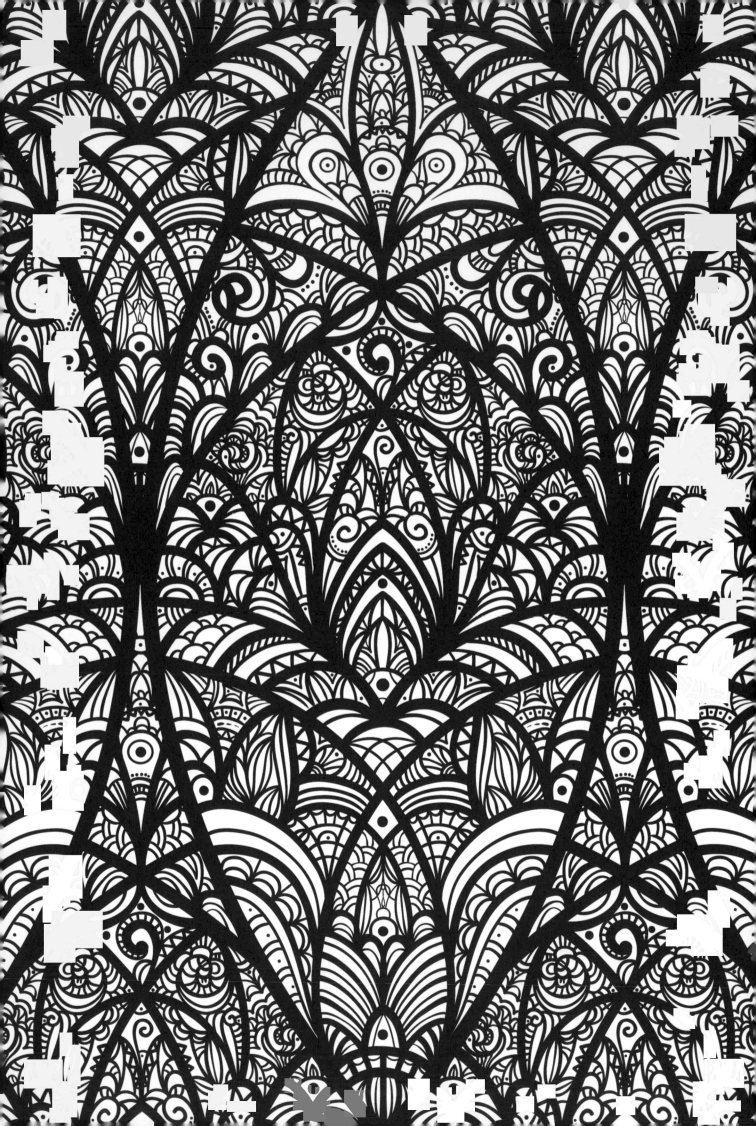

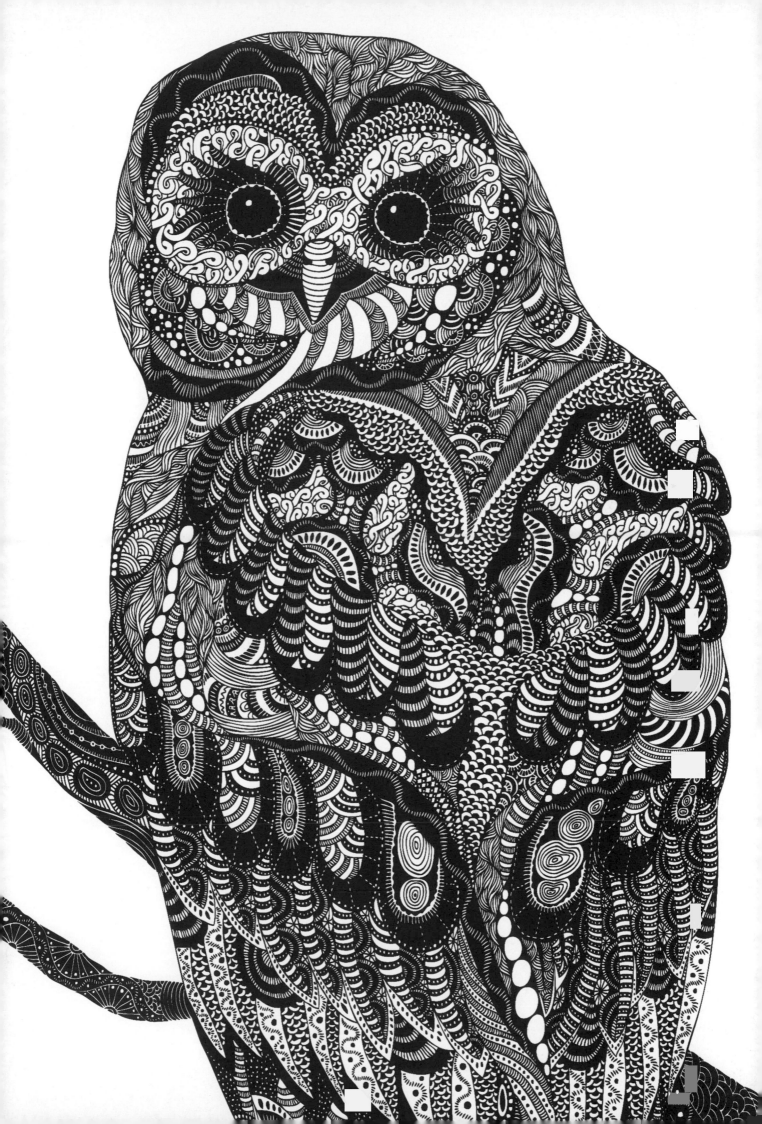

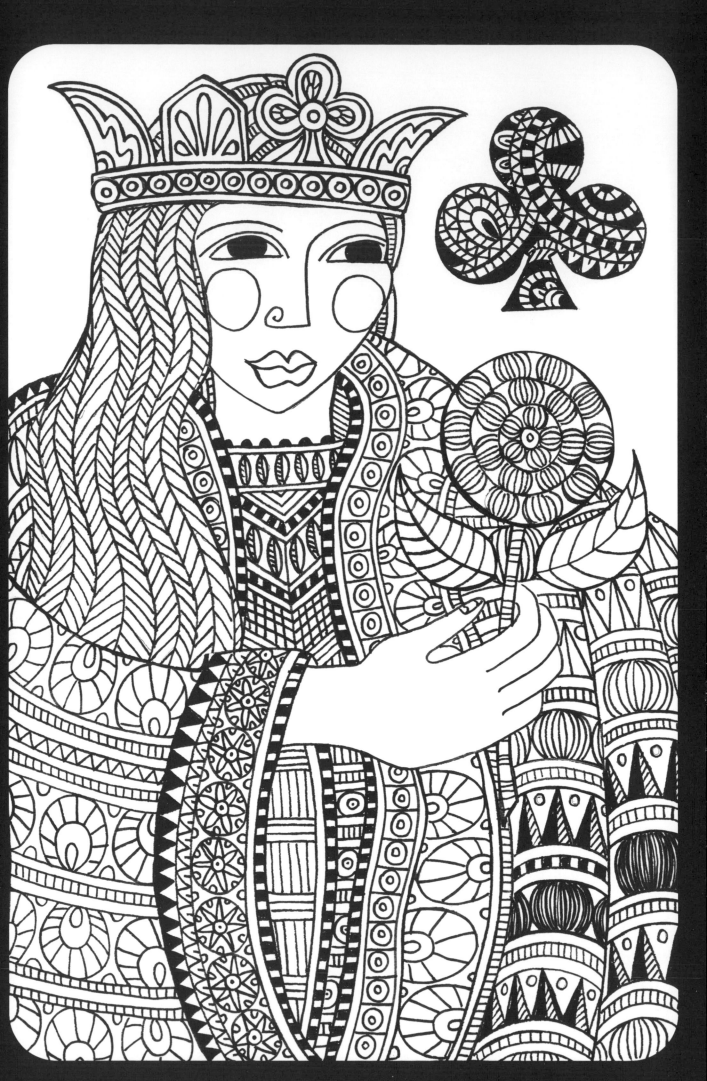

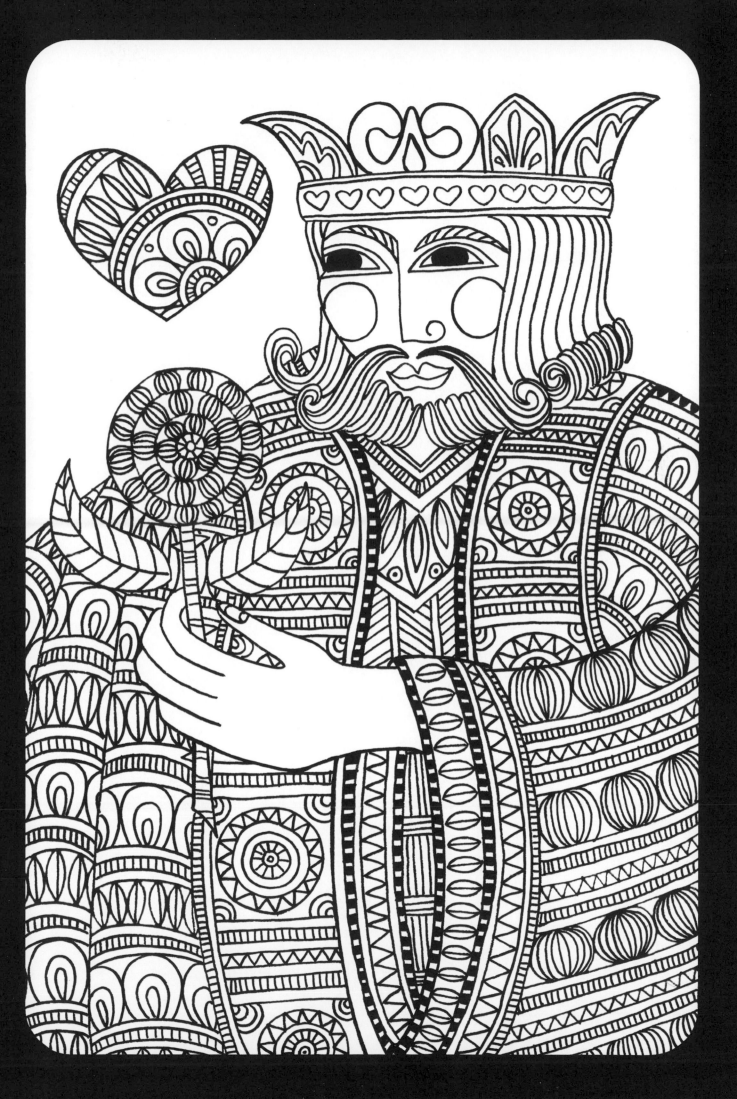

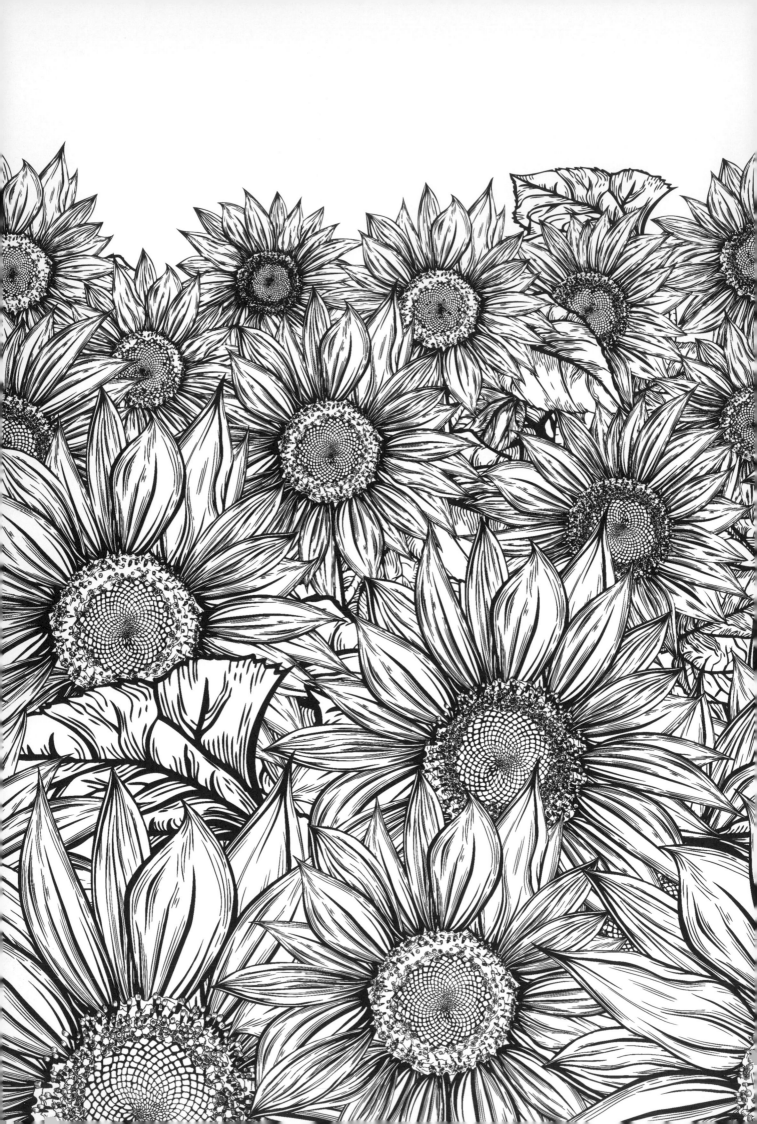

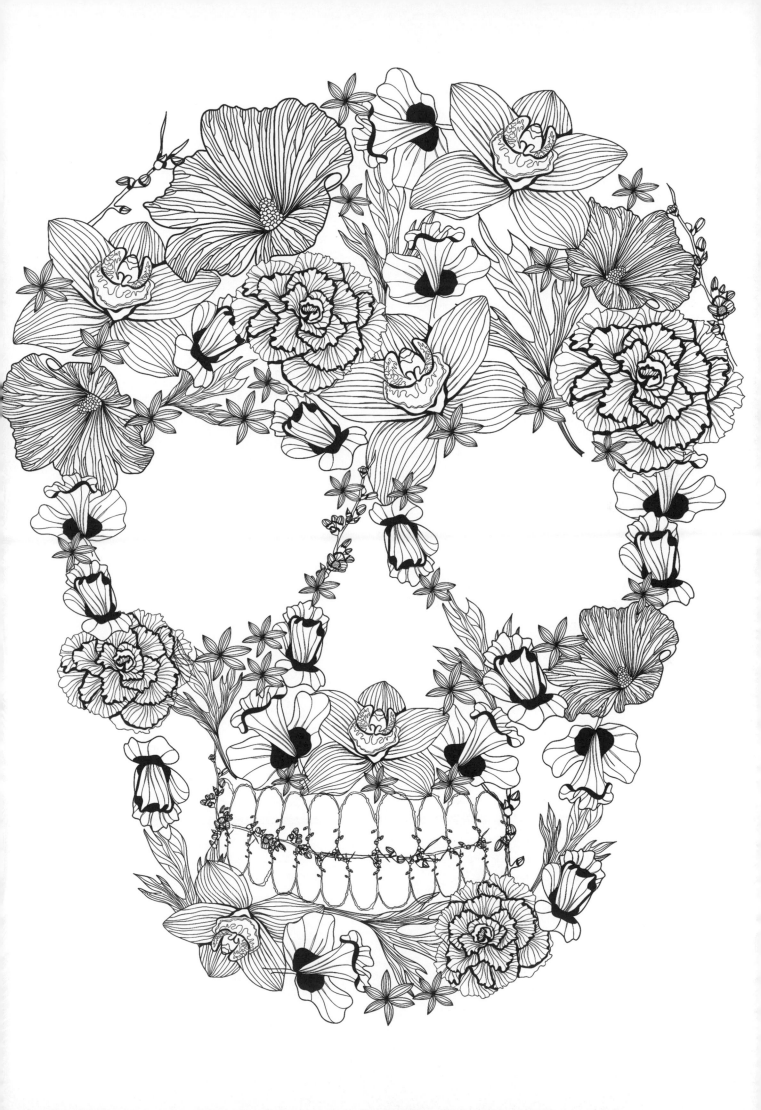

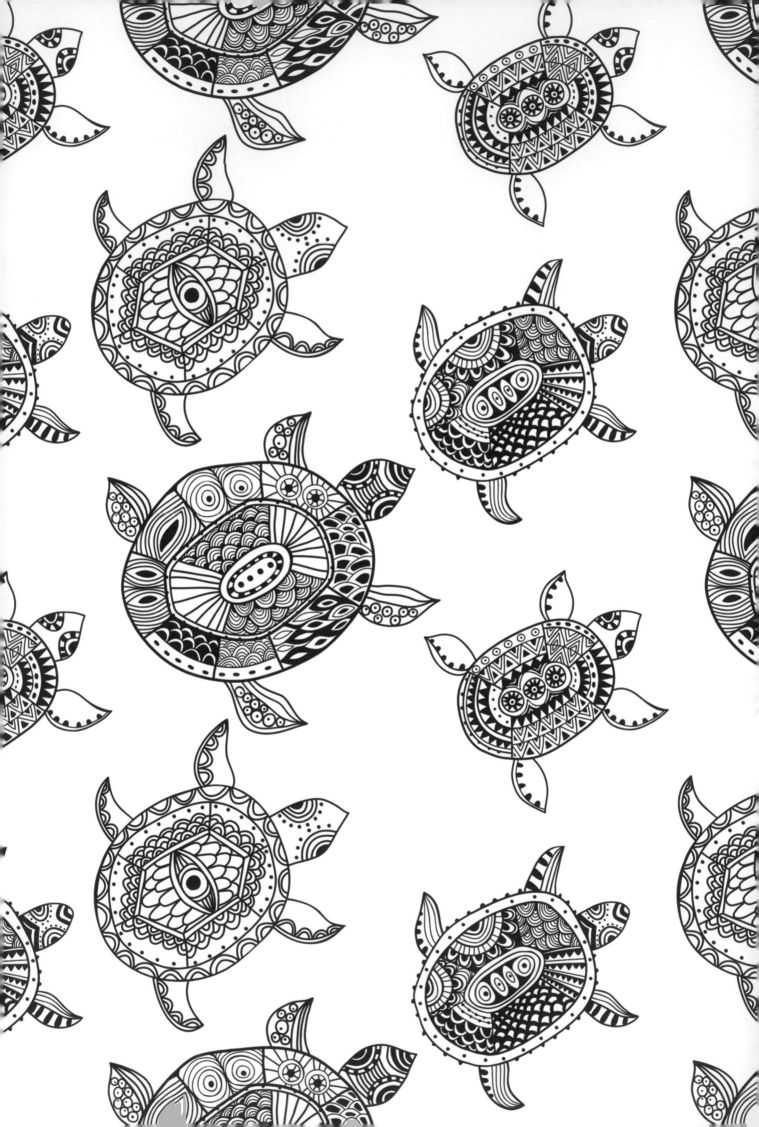

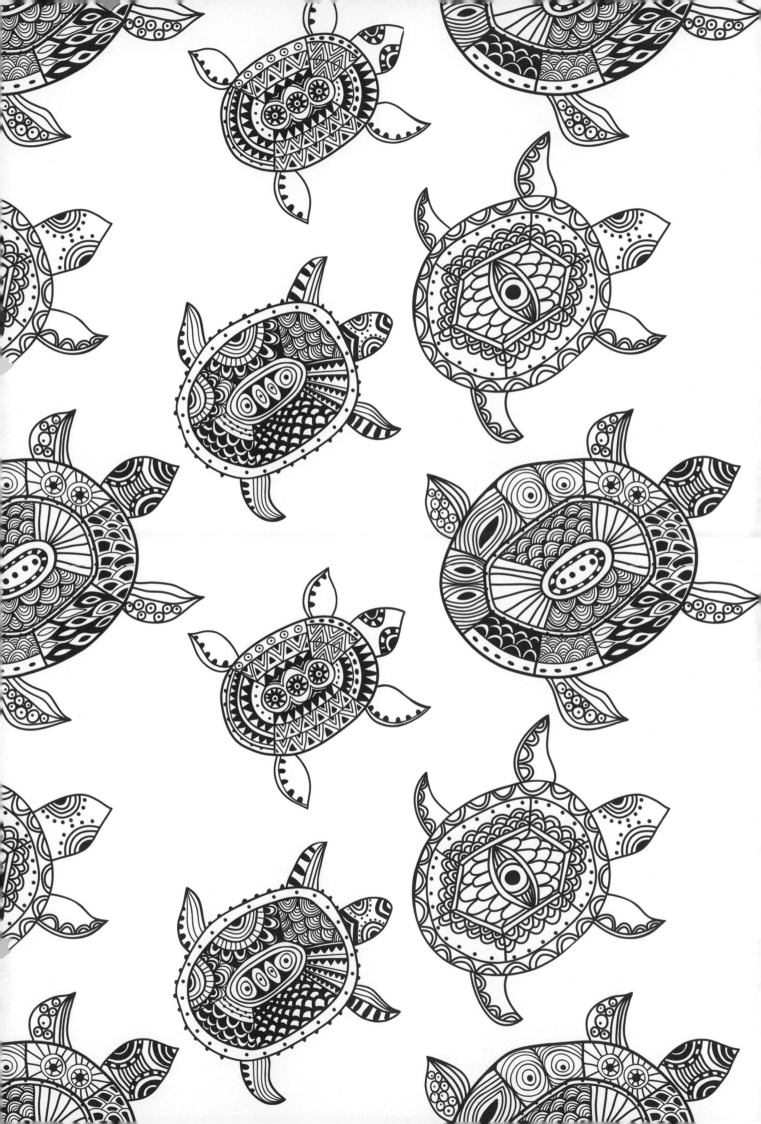

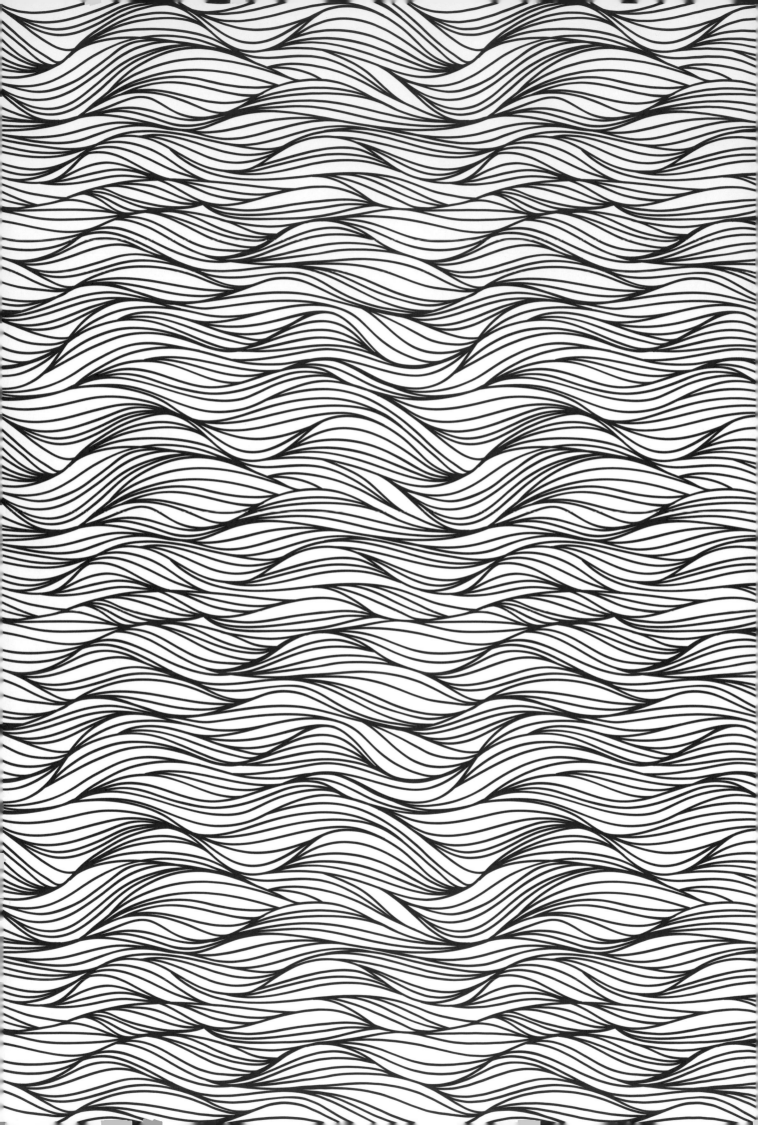

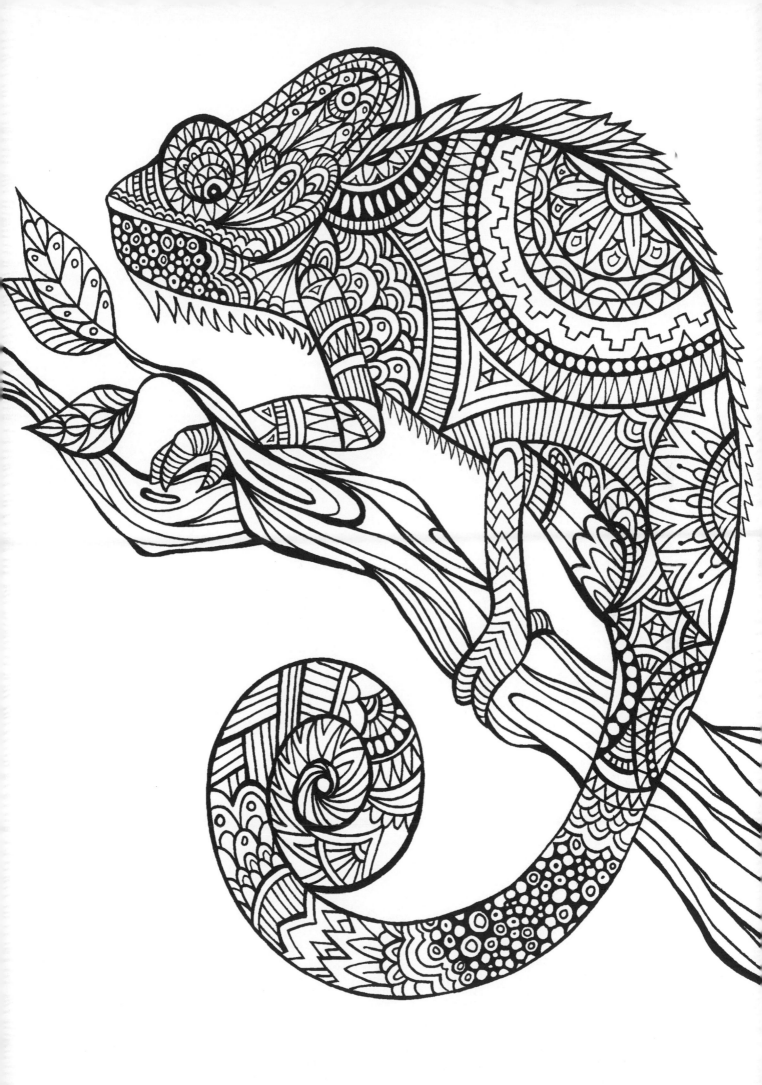

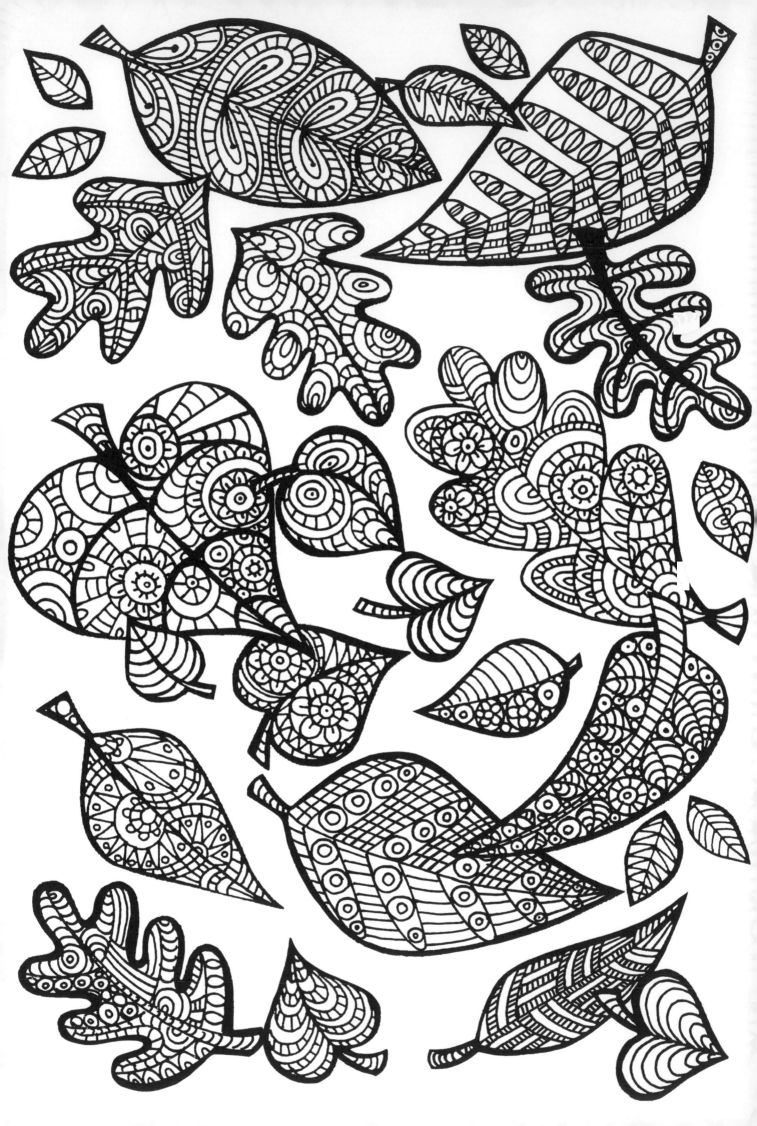

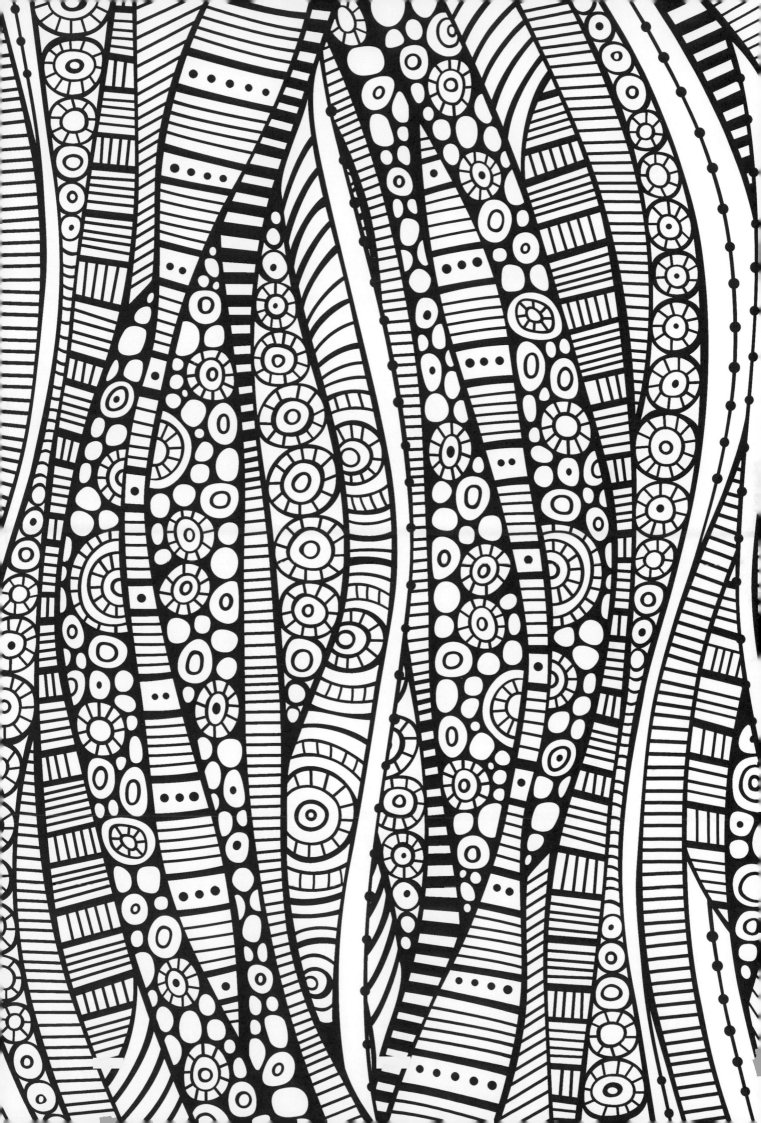

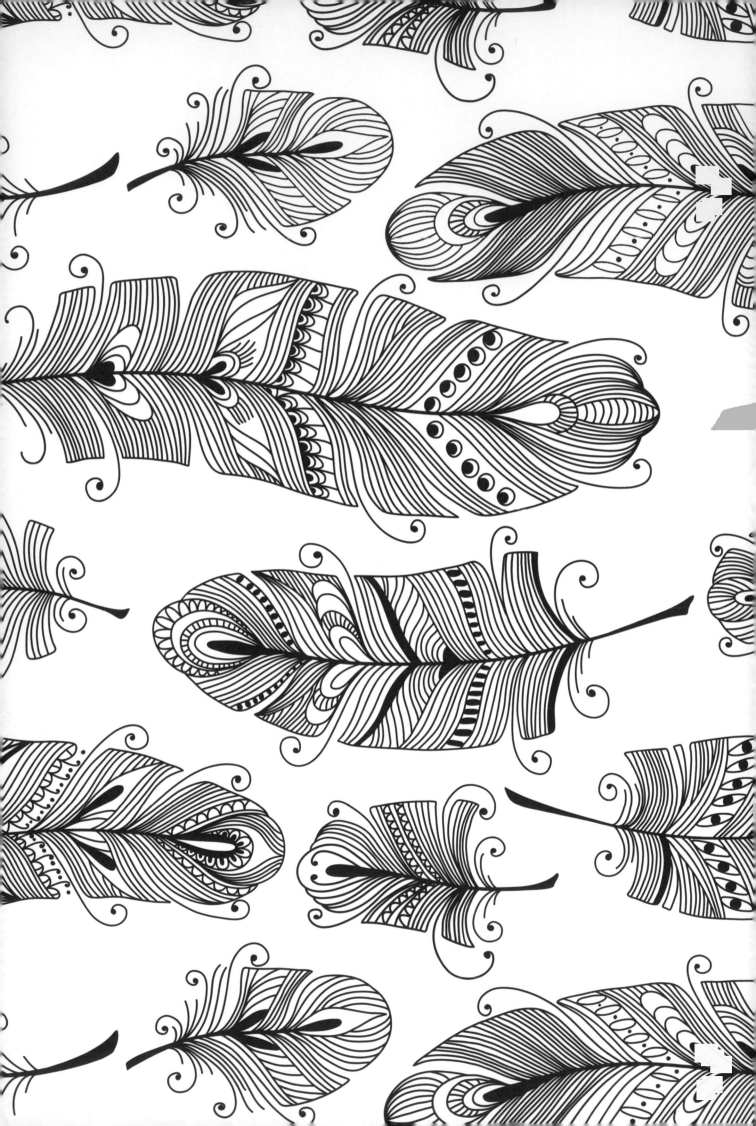

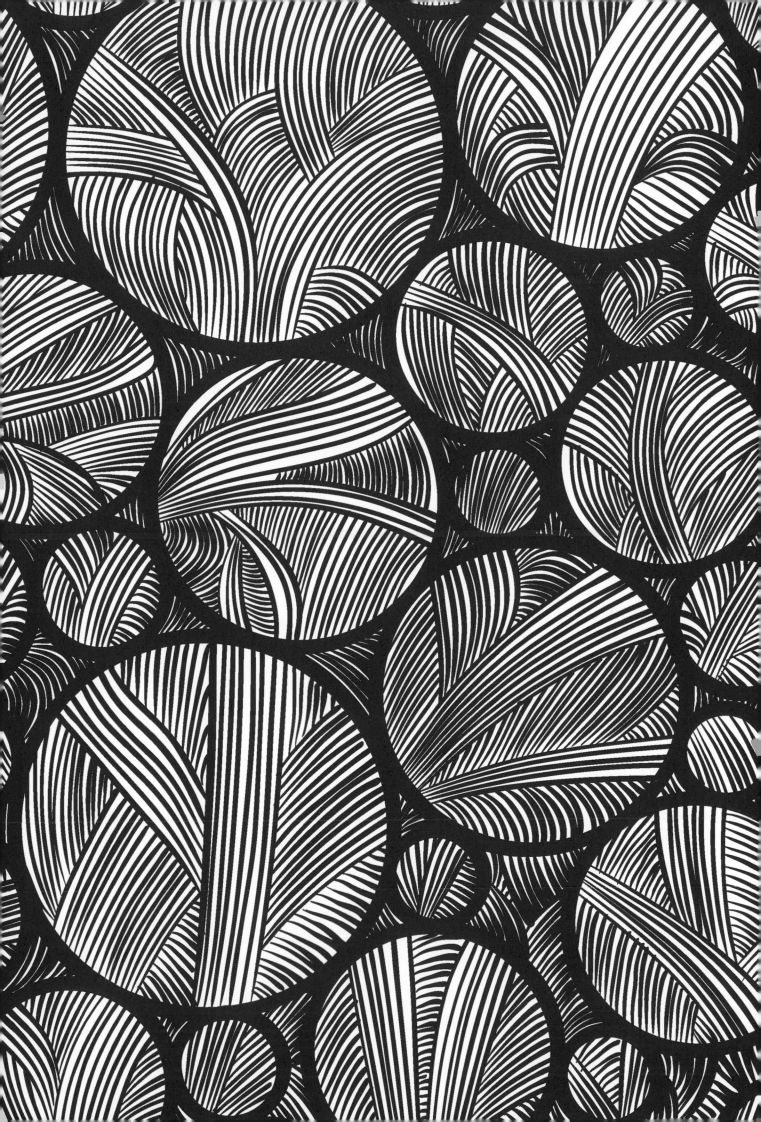

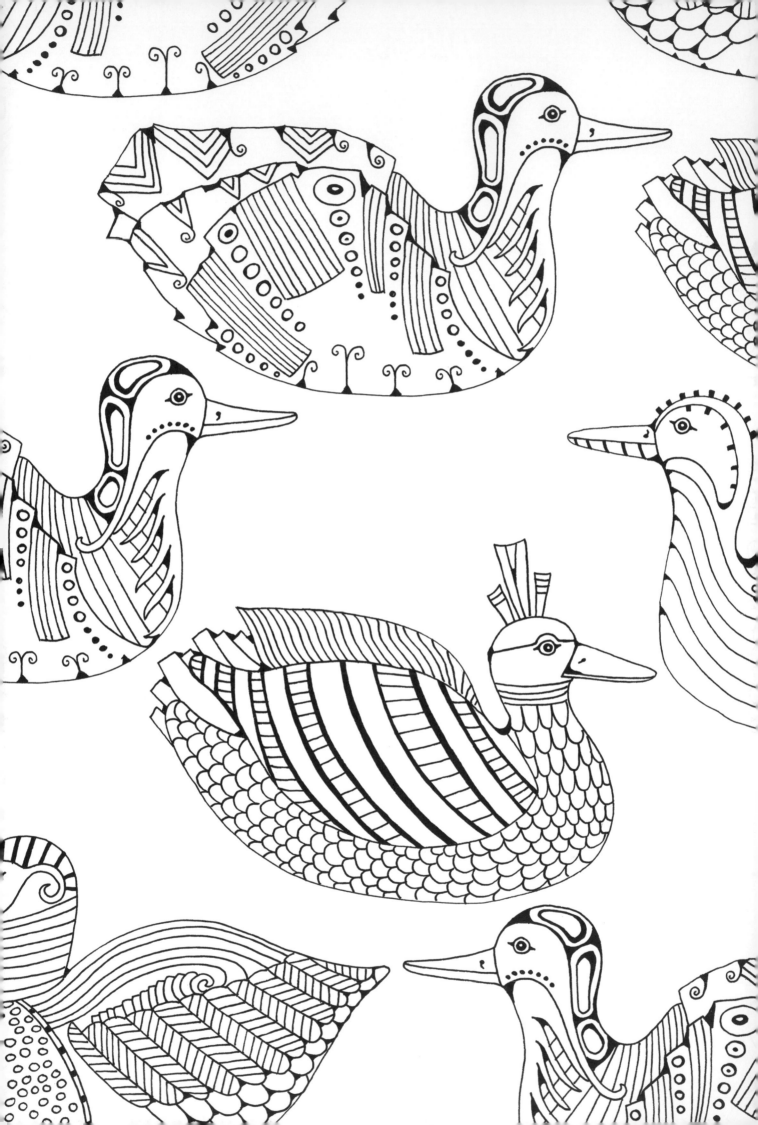

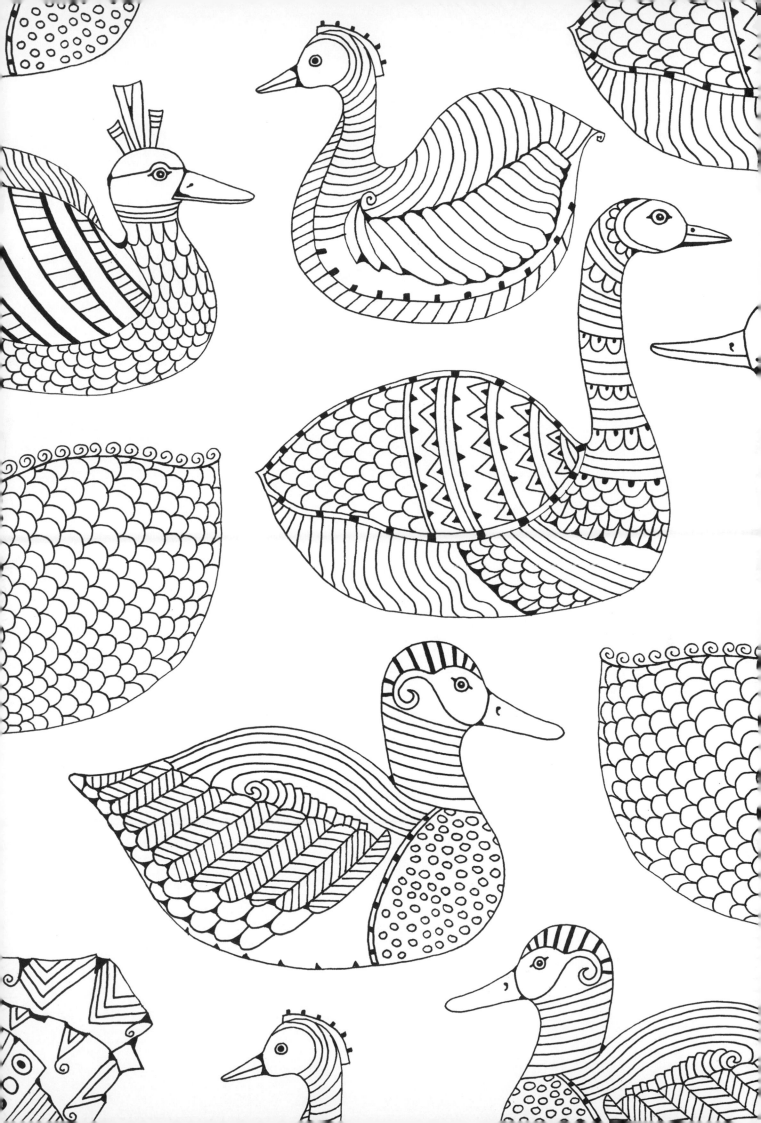

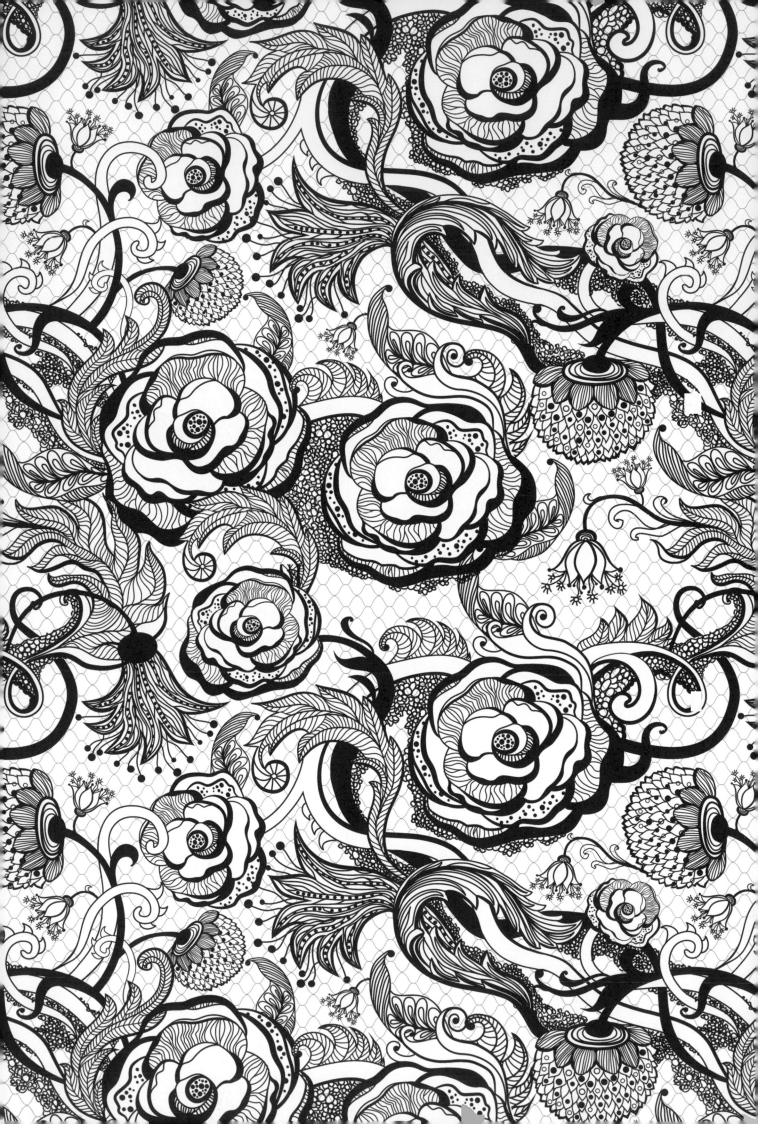

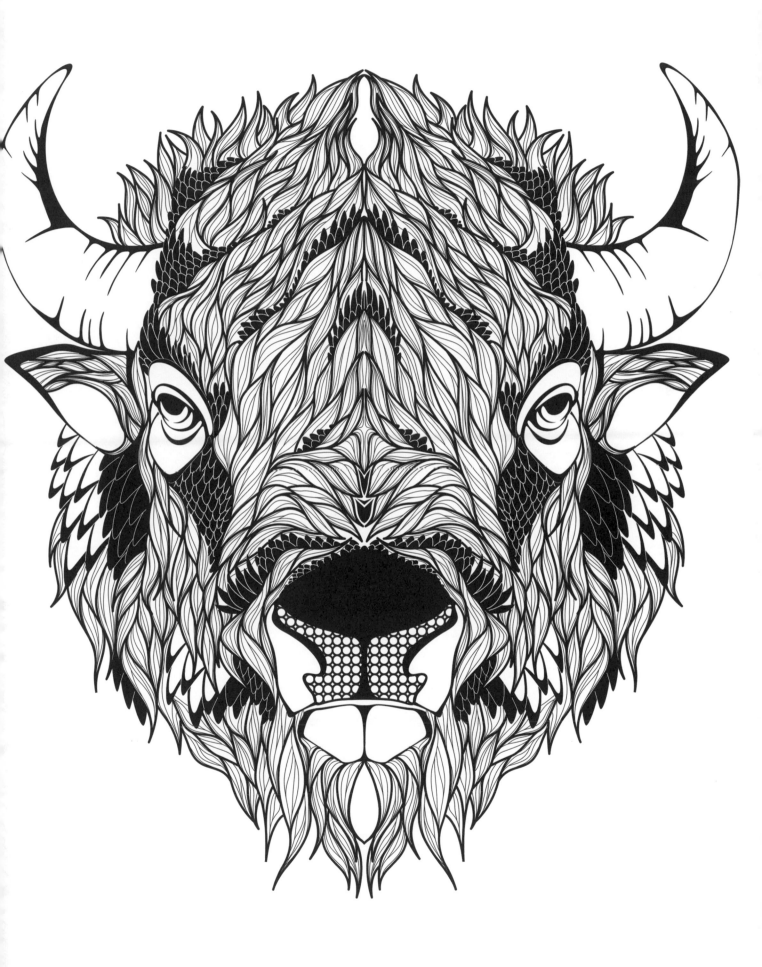

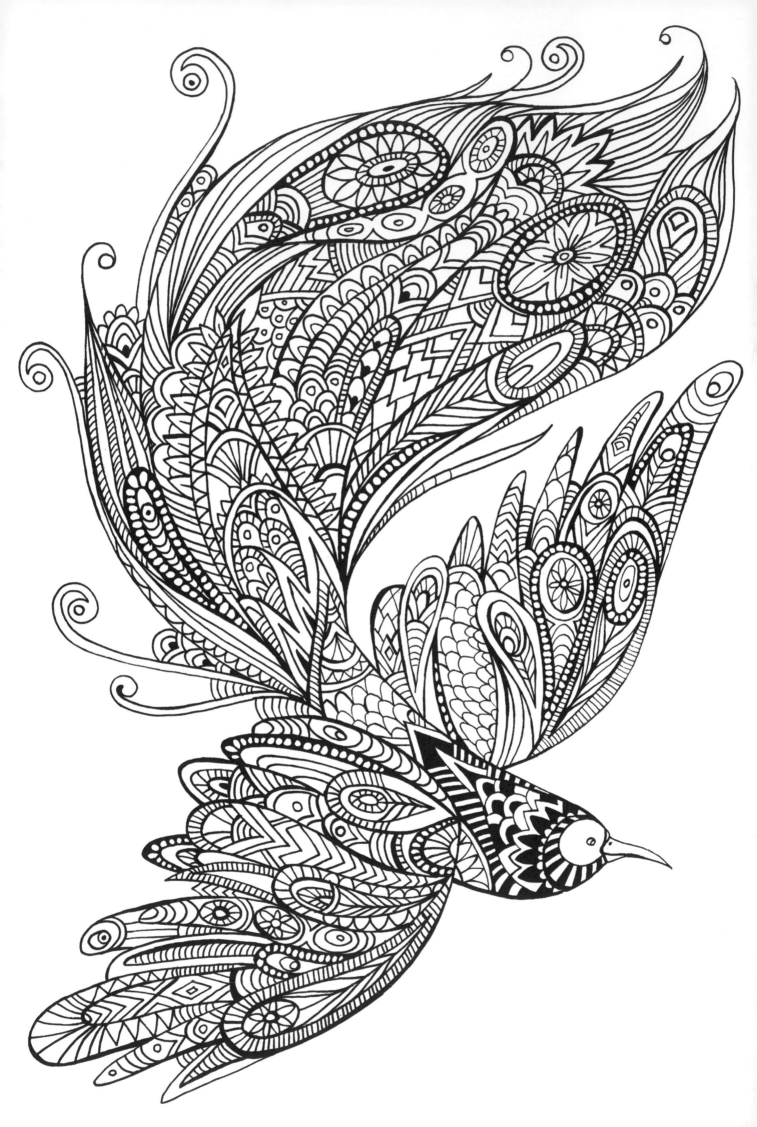

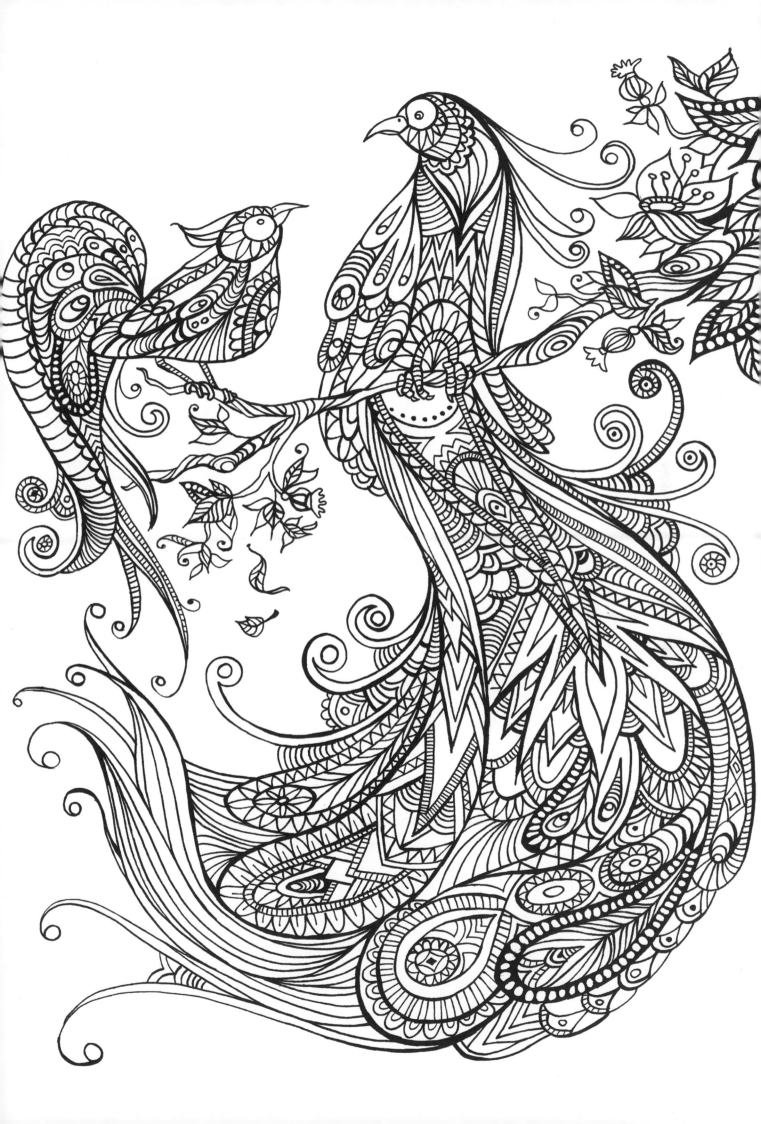

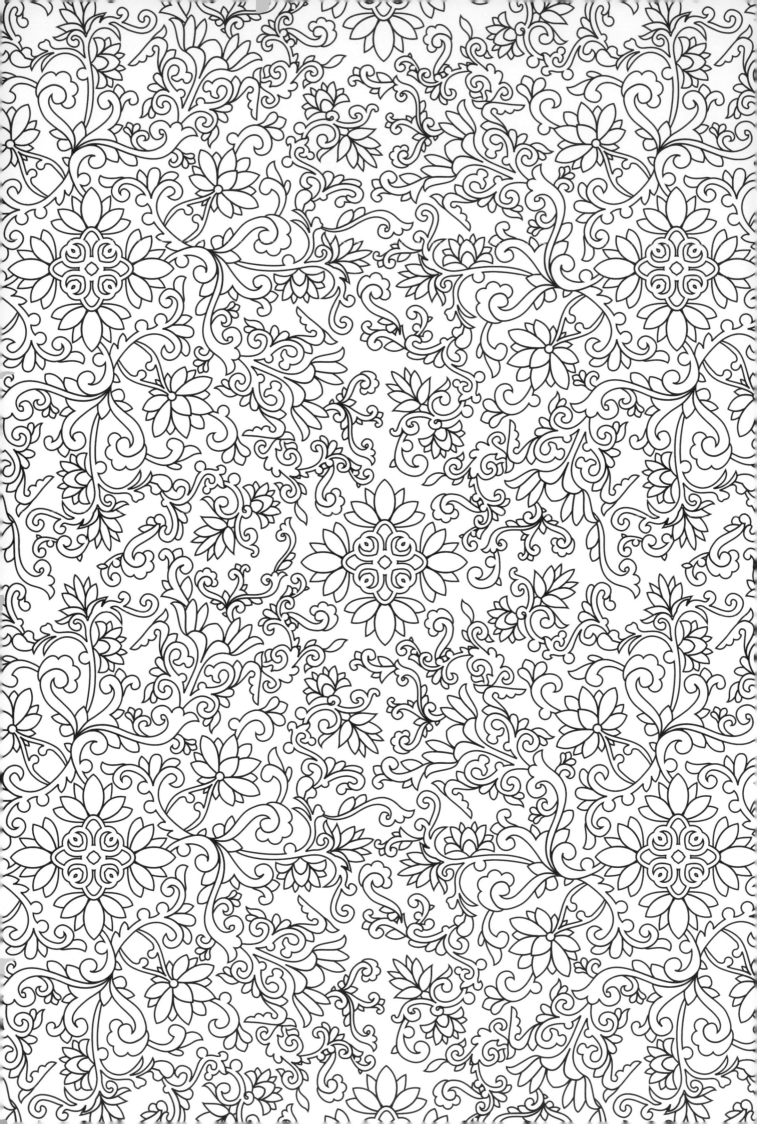

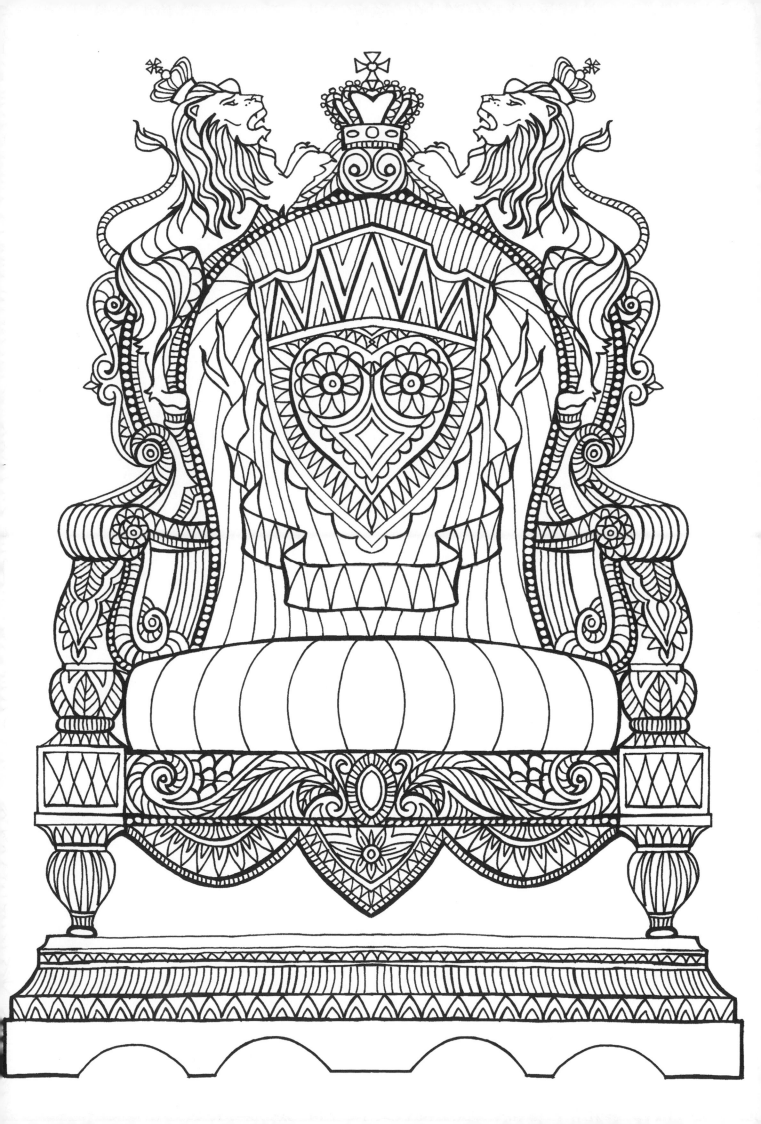

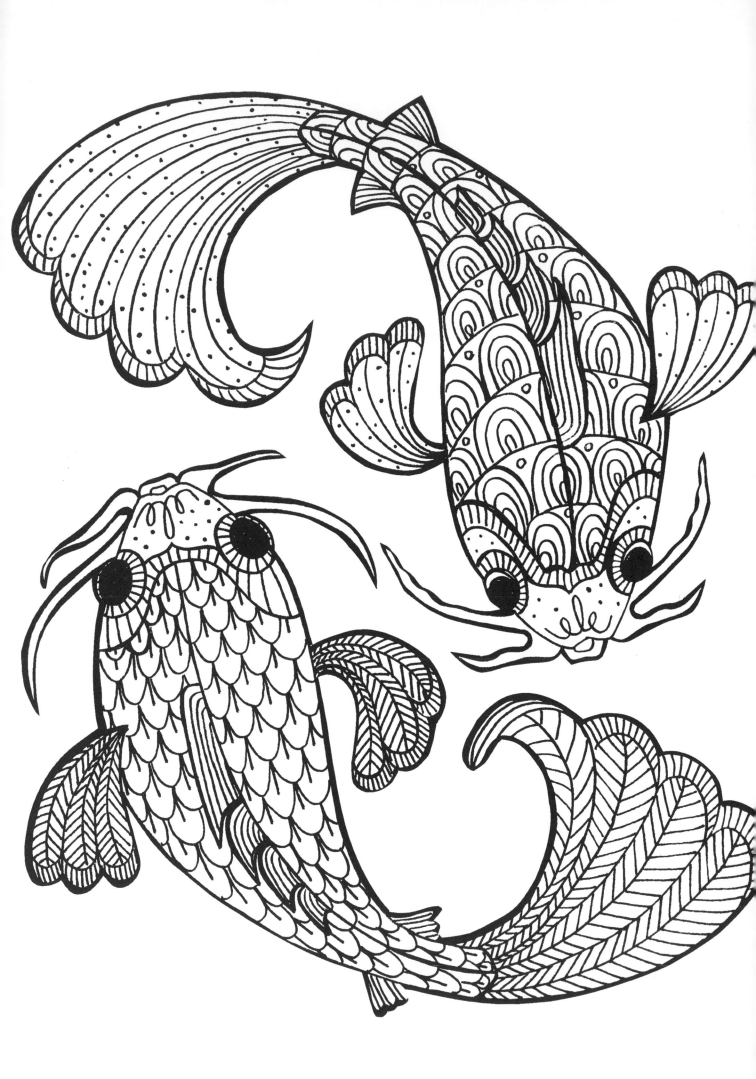

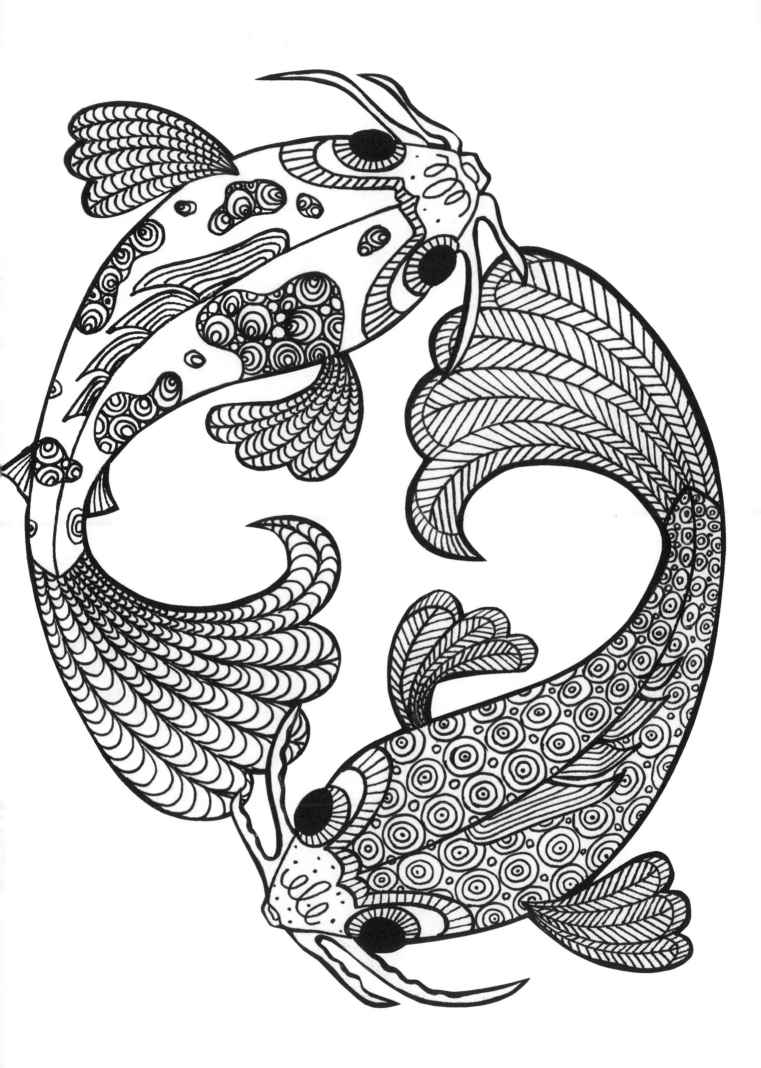

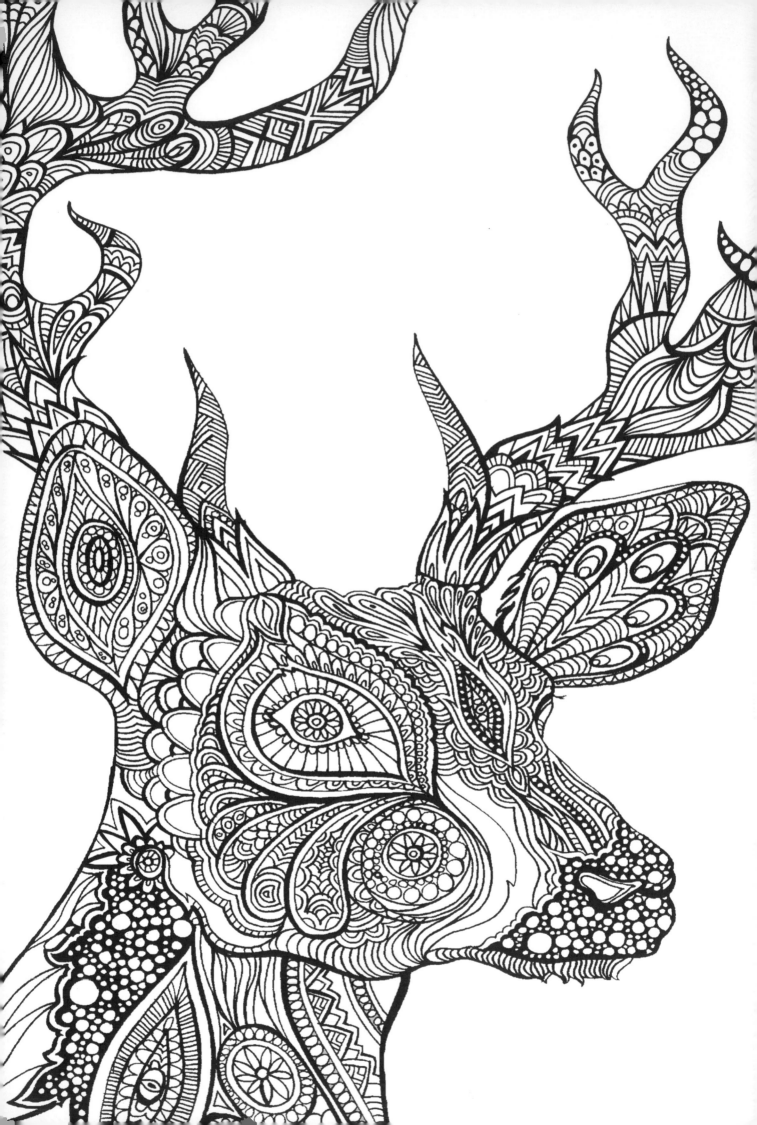

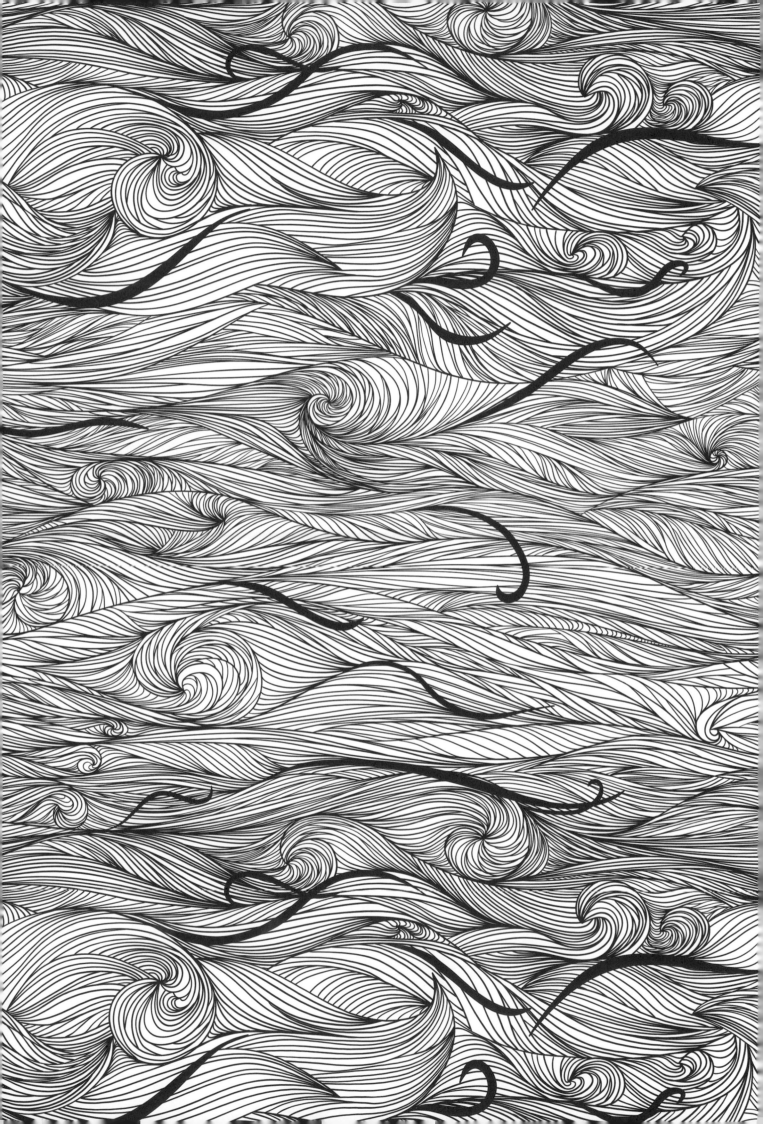

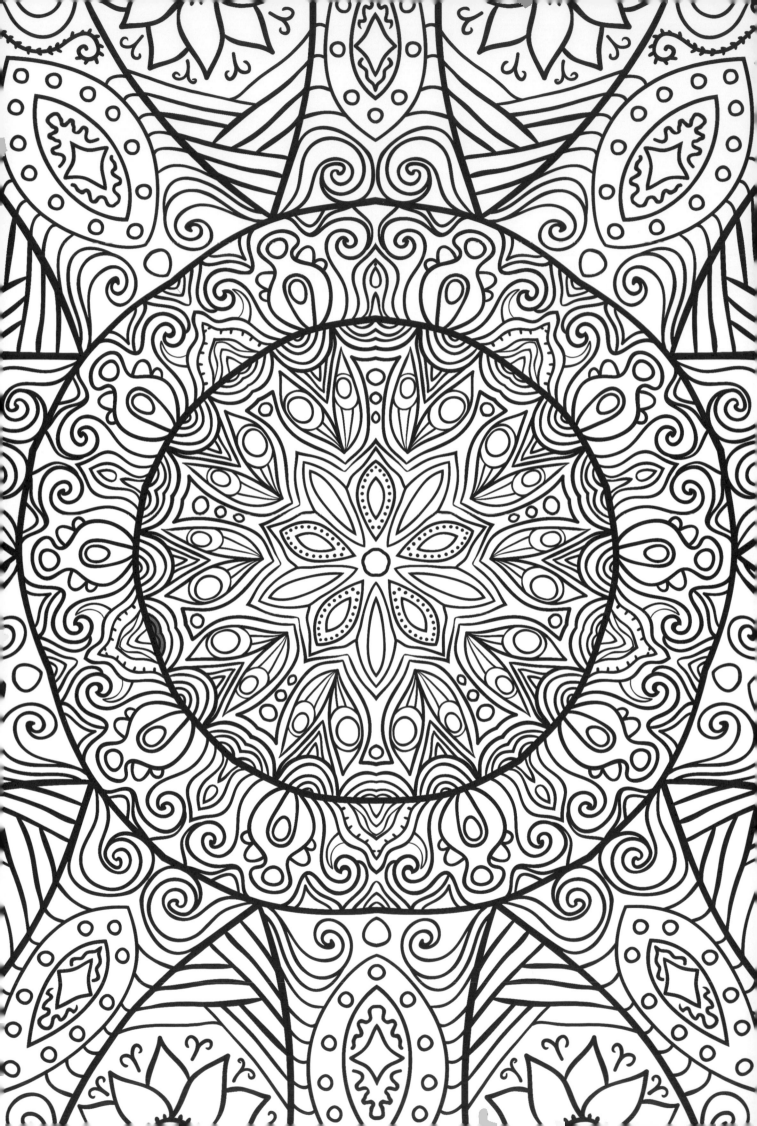

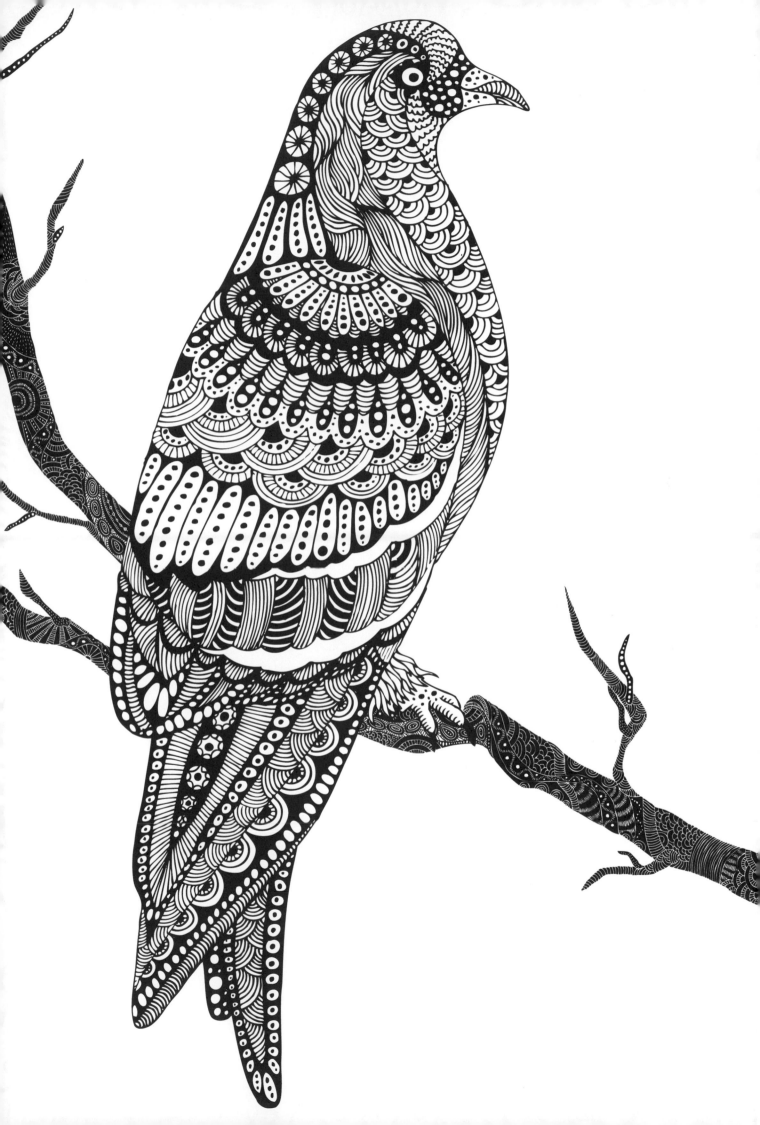

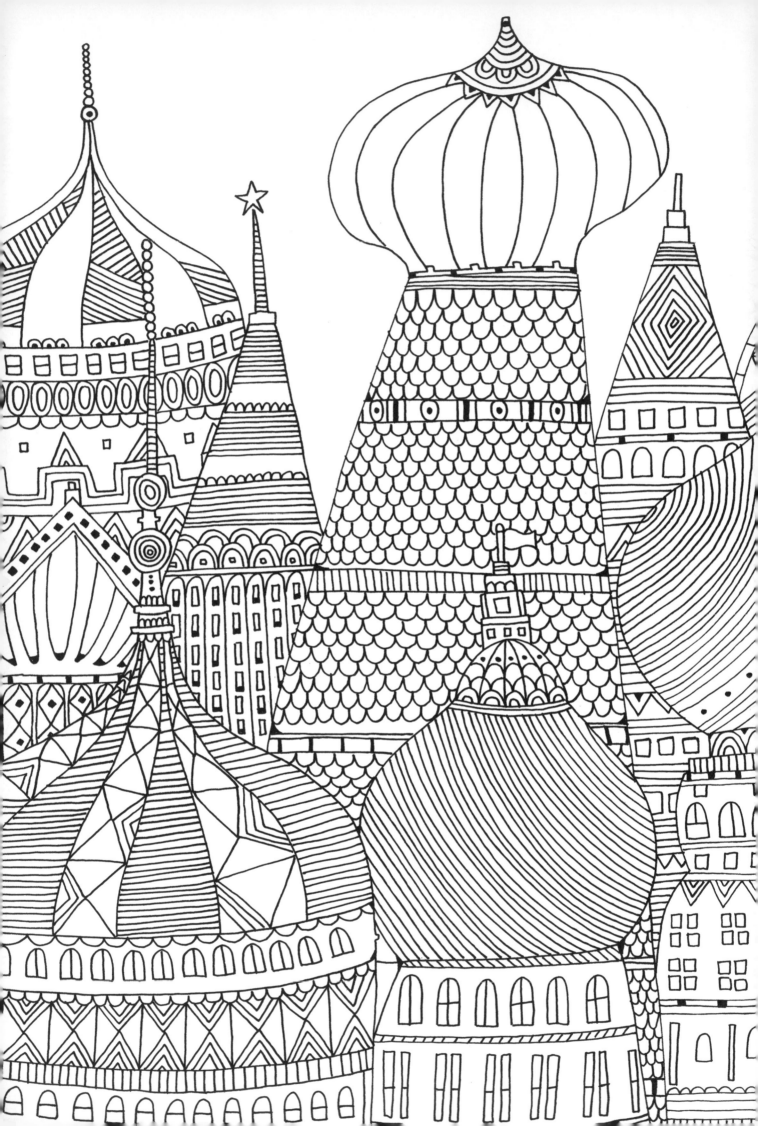

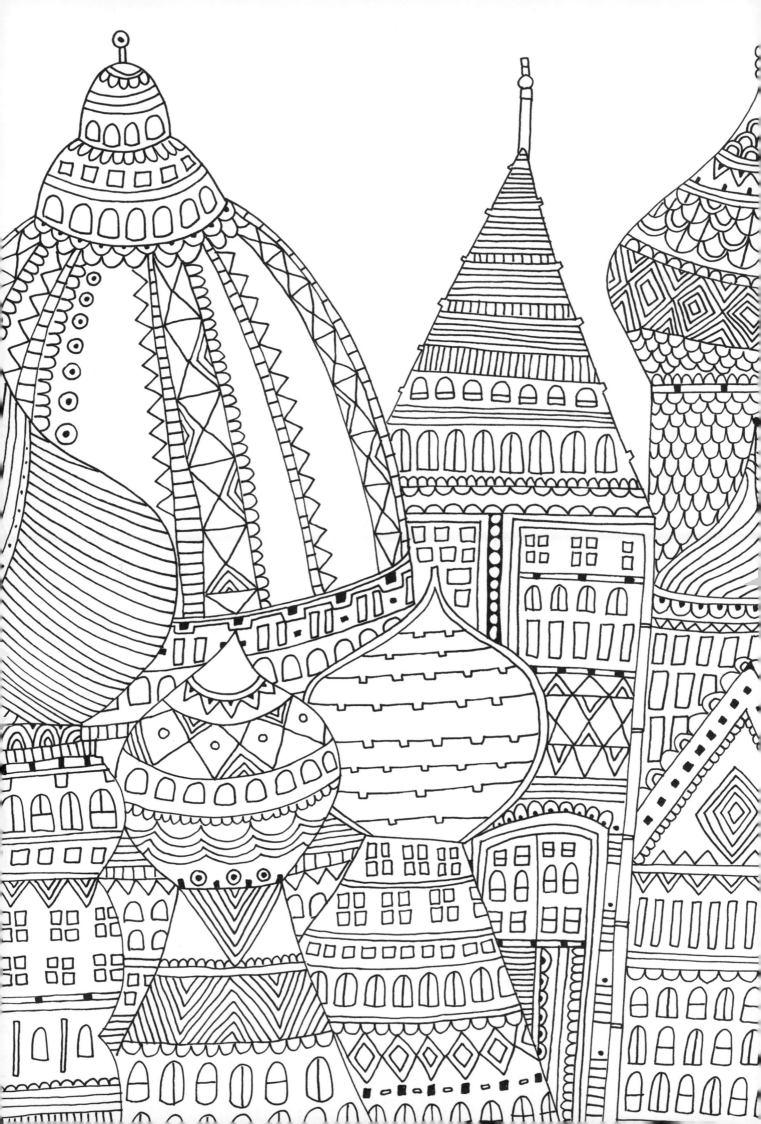

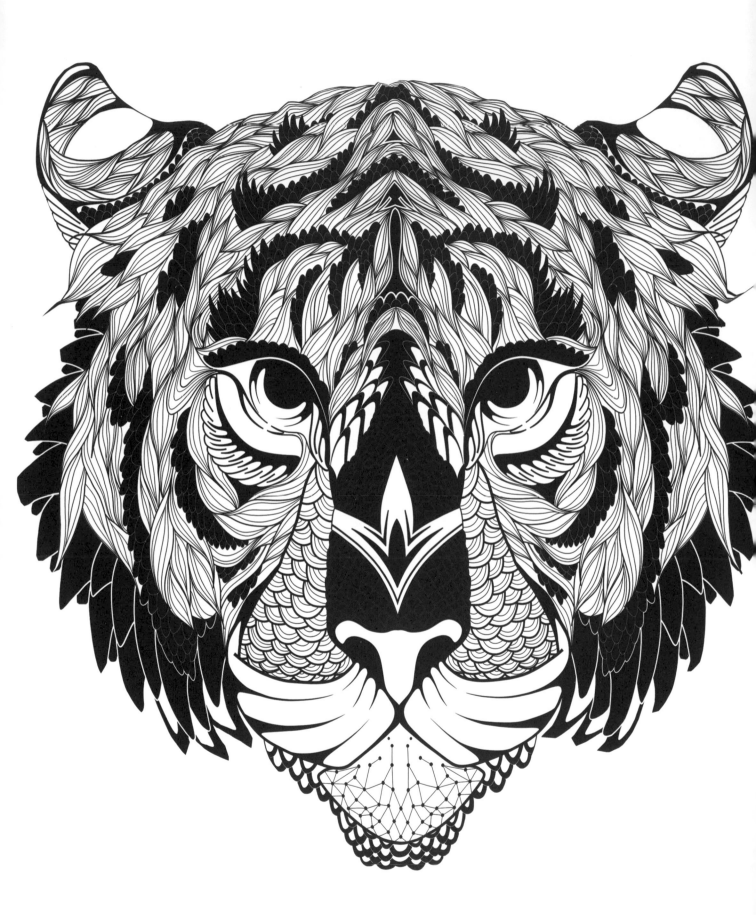

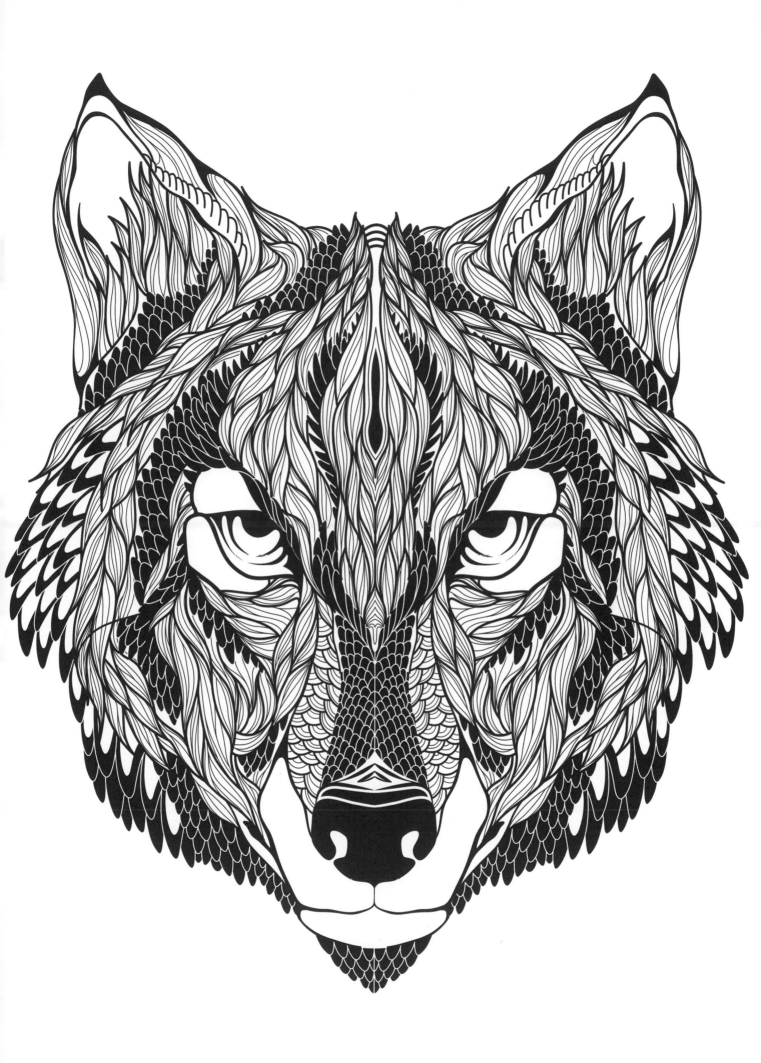

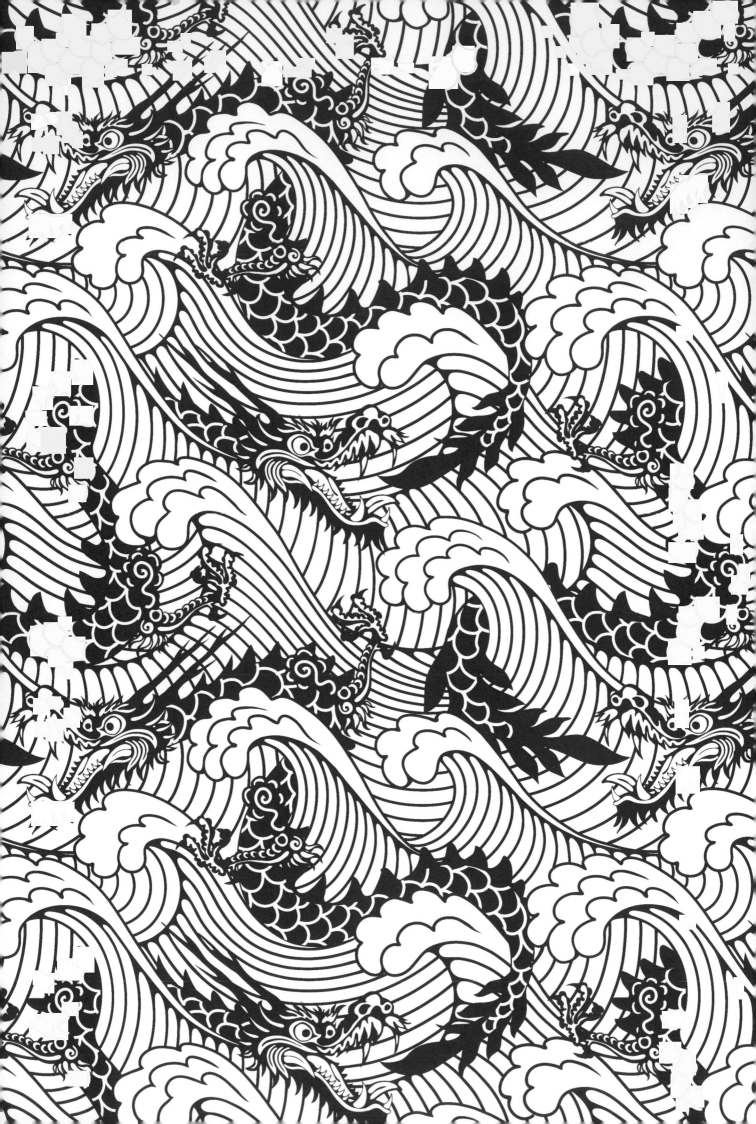

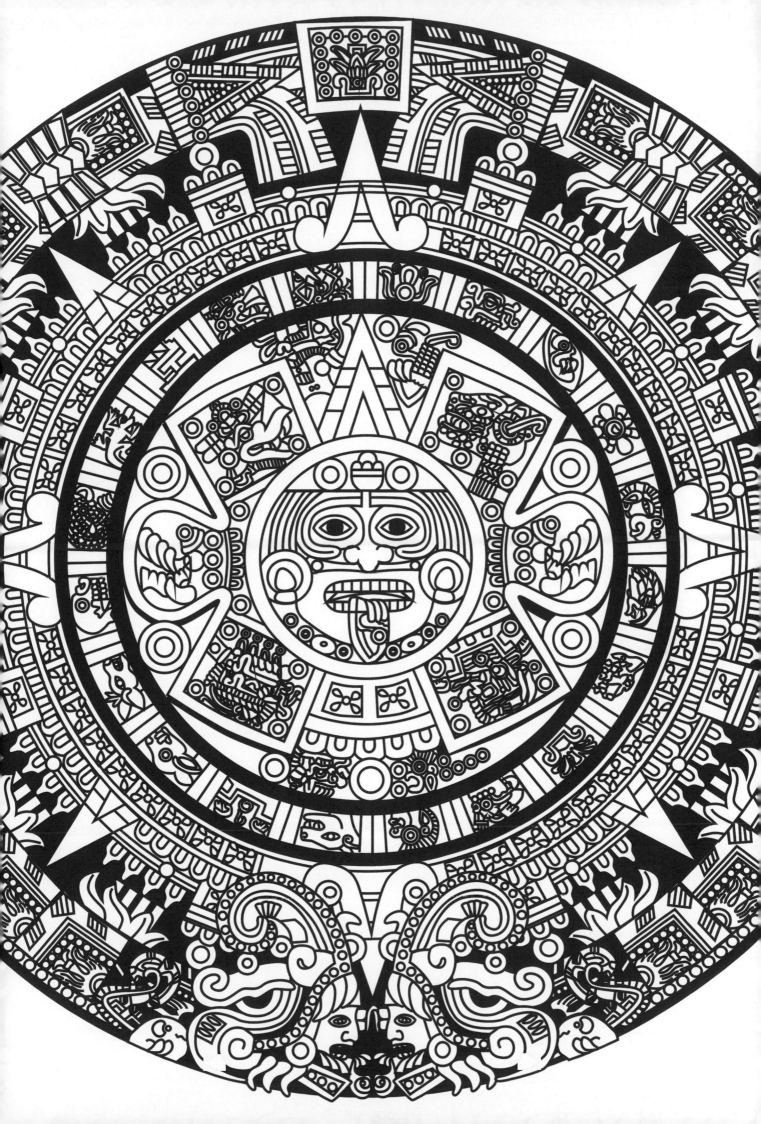

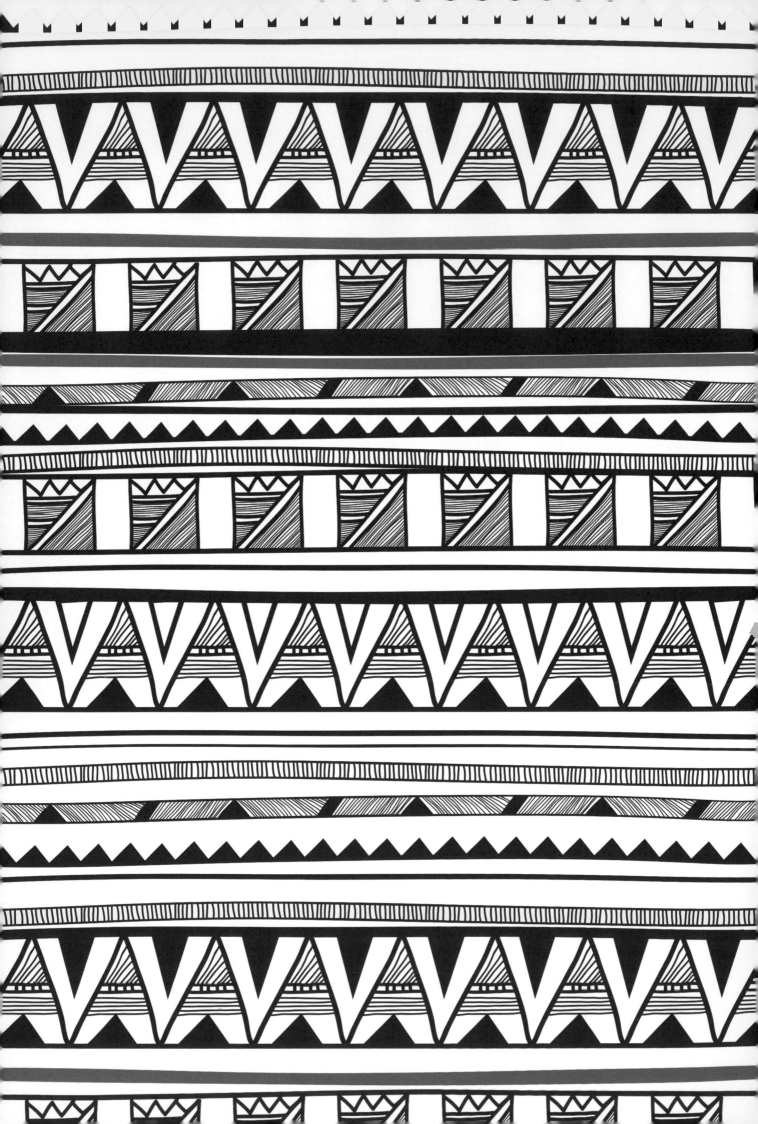

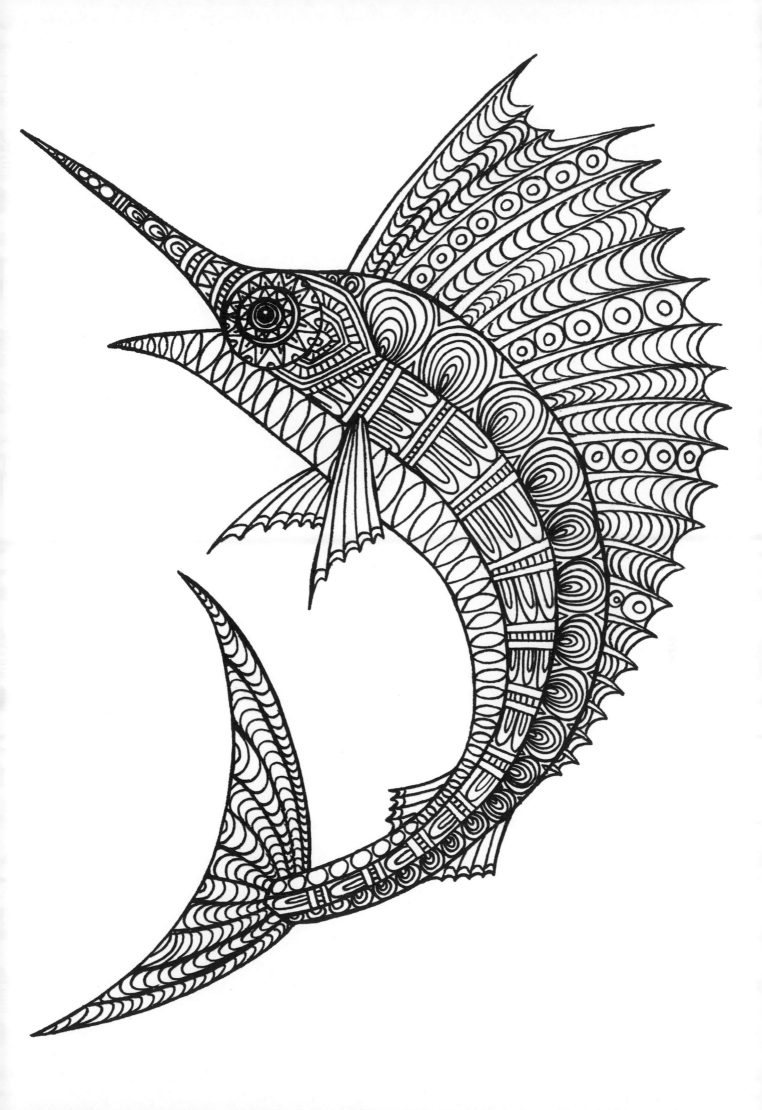

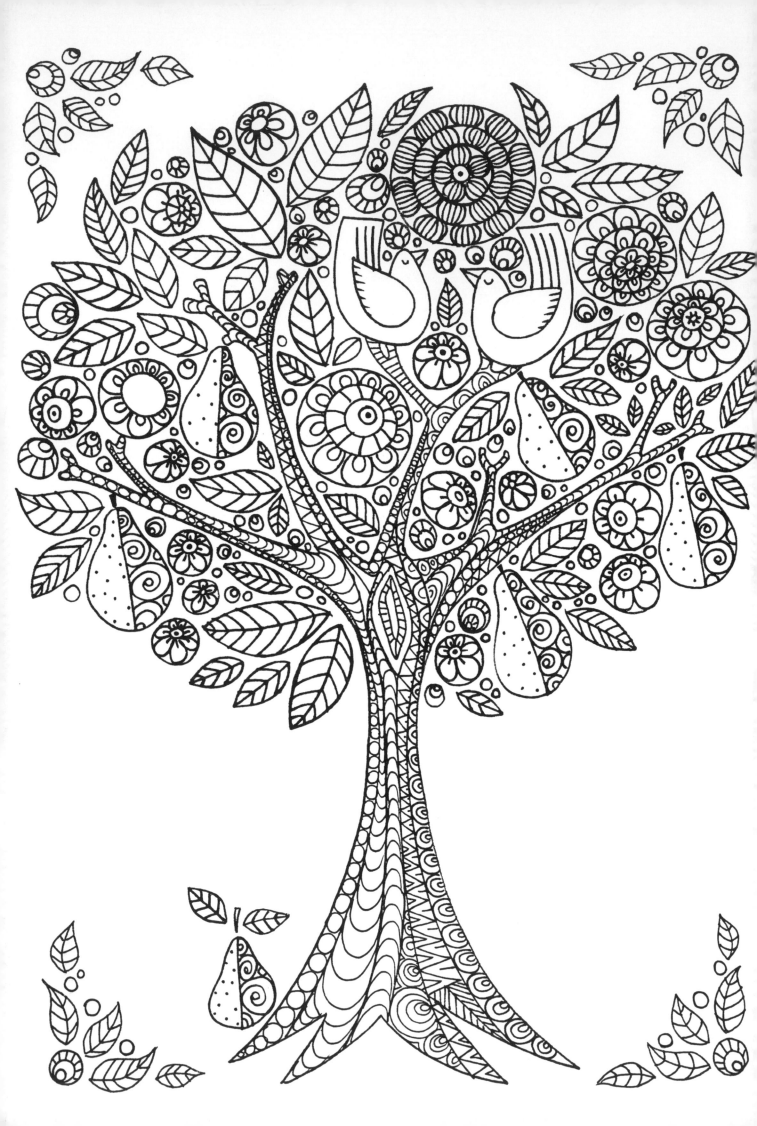

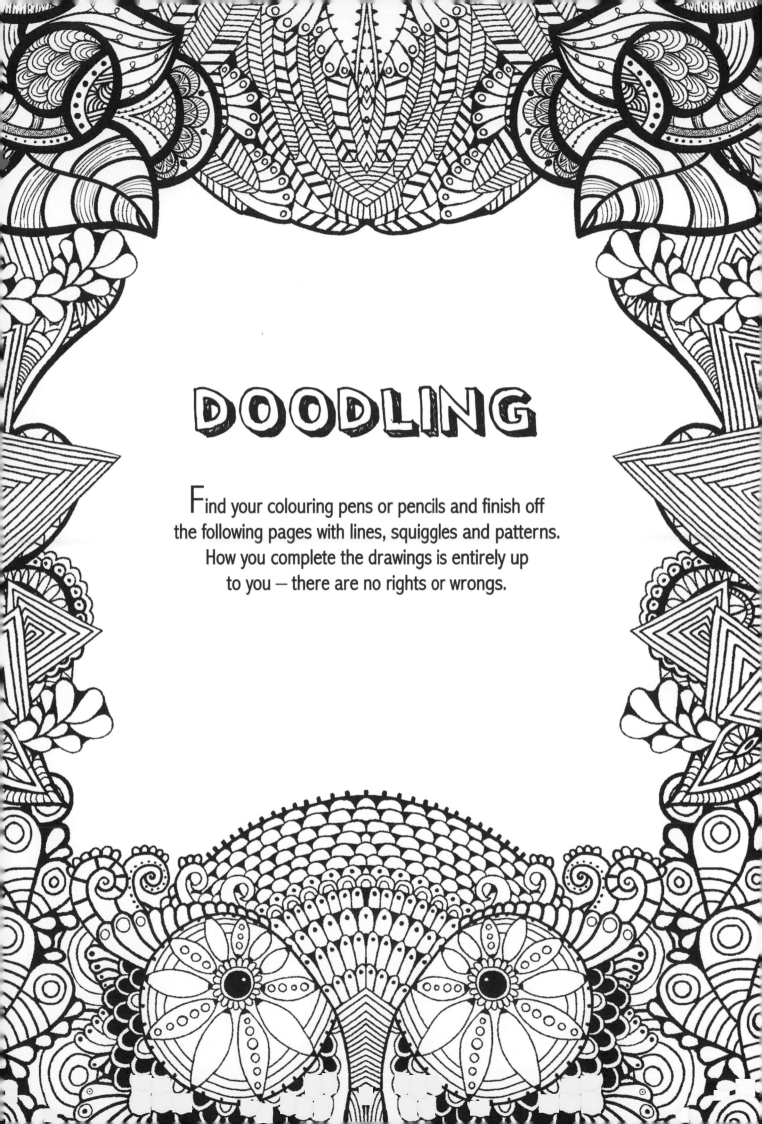

DOODLING

Find your colouring pens or pencils and finish off
the following pages with lines, squiggles and patterns.
How you complete the drawings is entirely up
to you — there are no rights or wrongs.

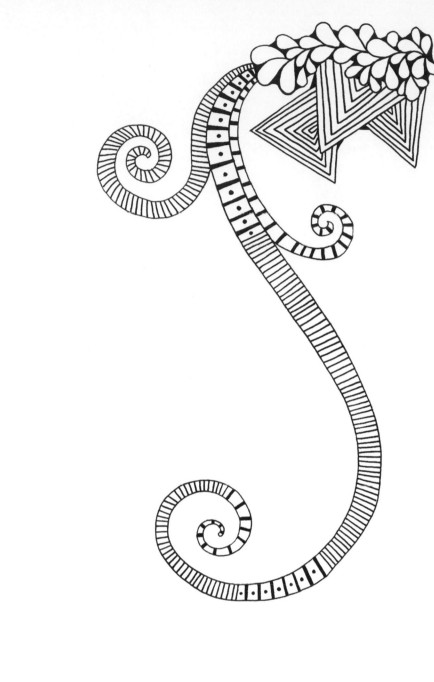
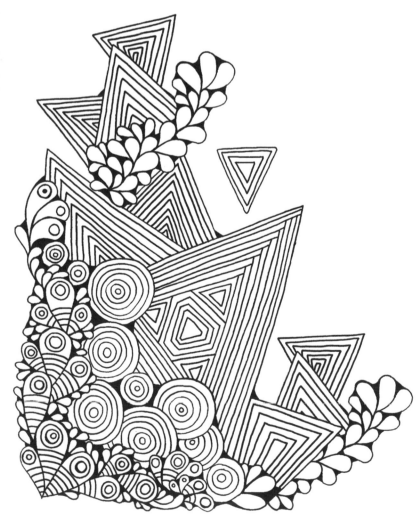

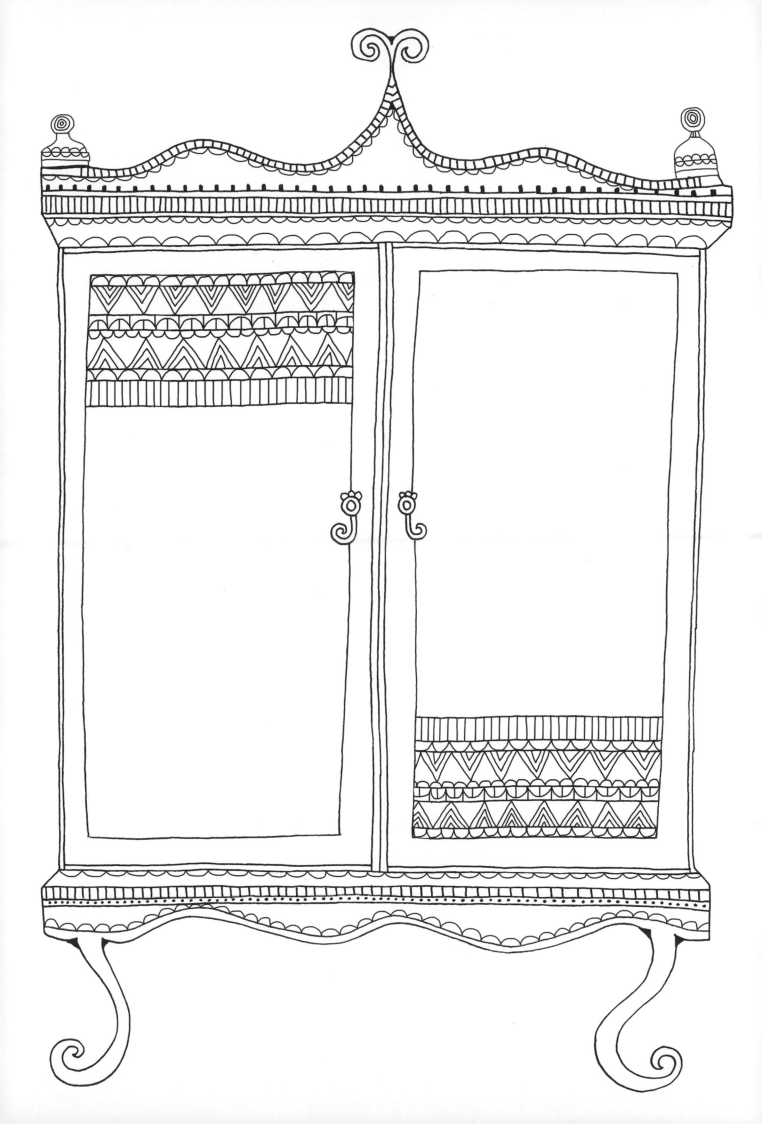

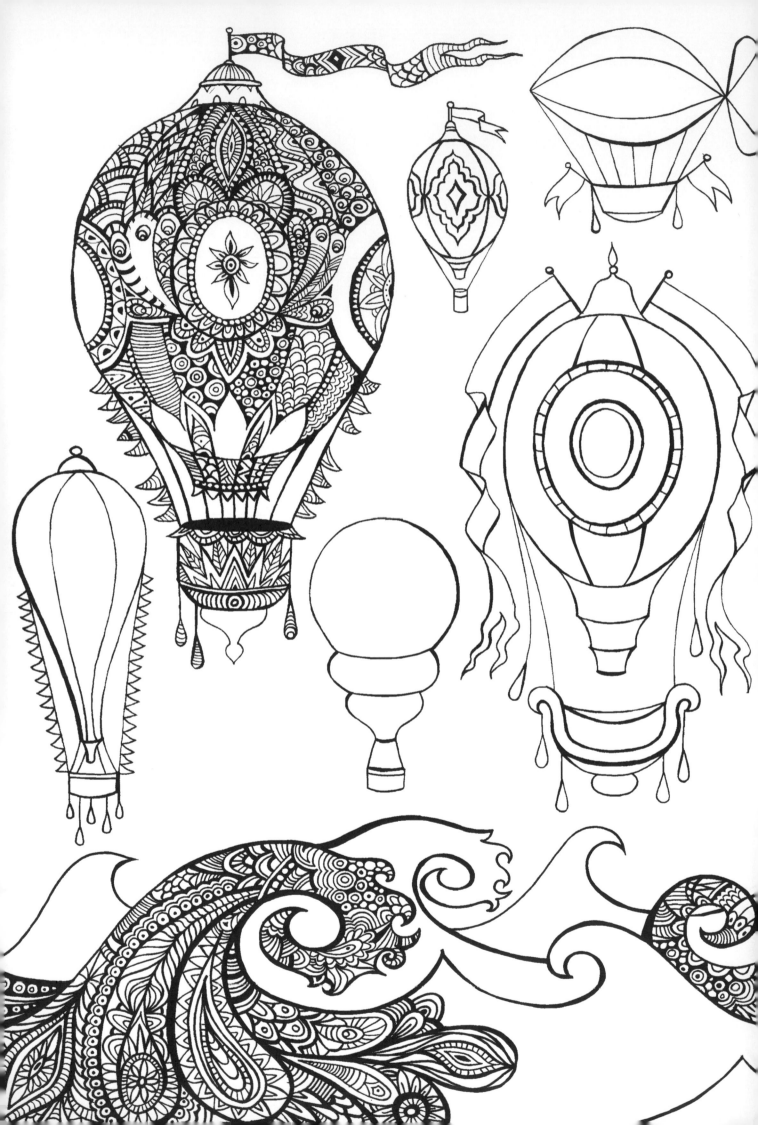

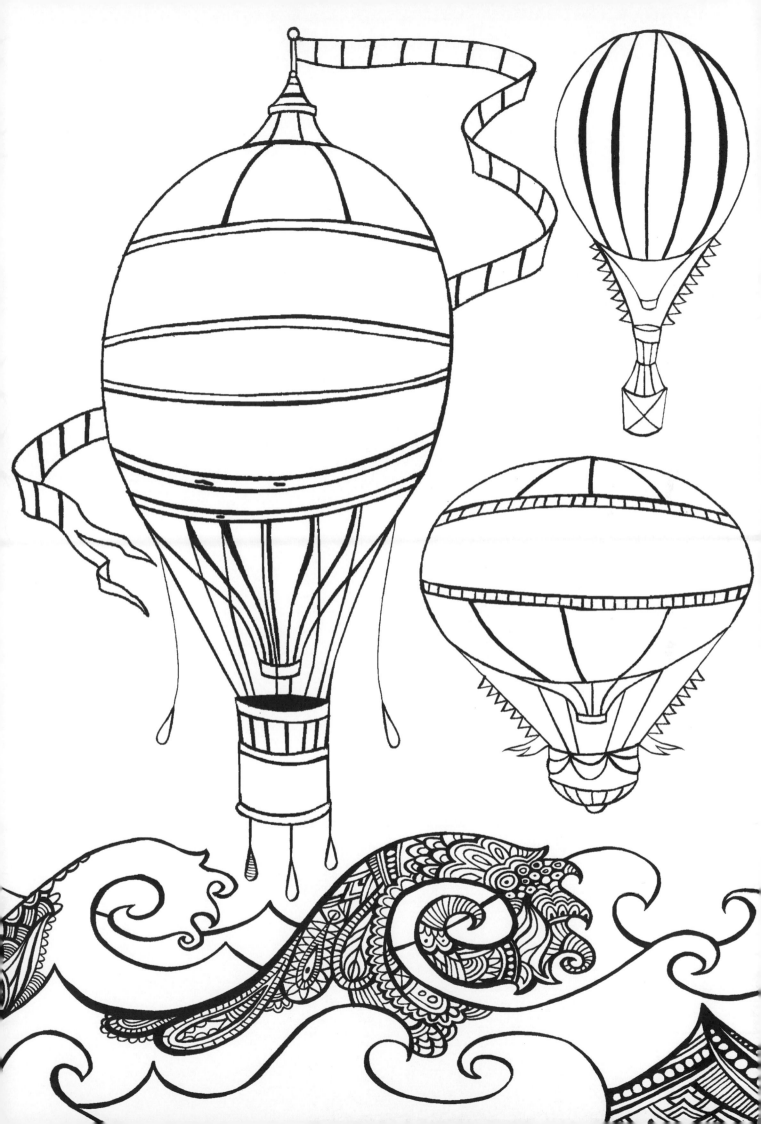

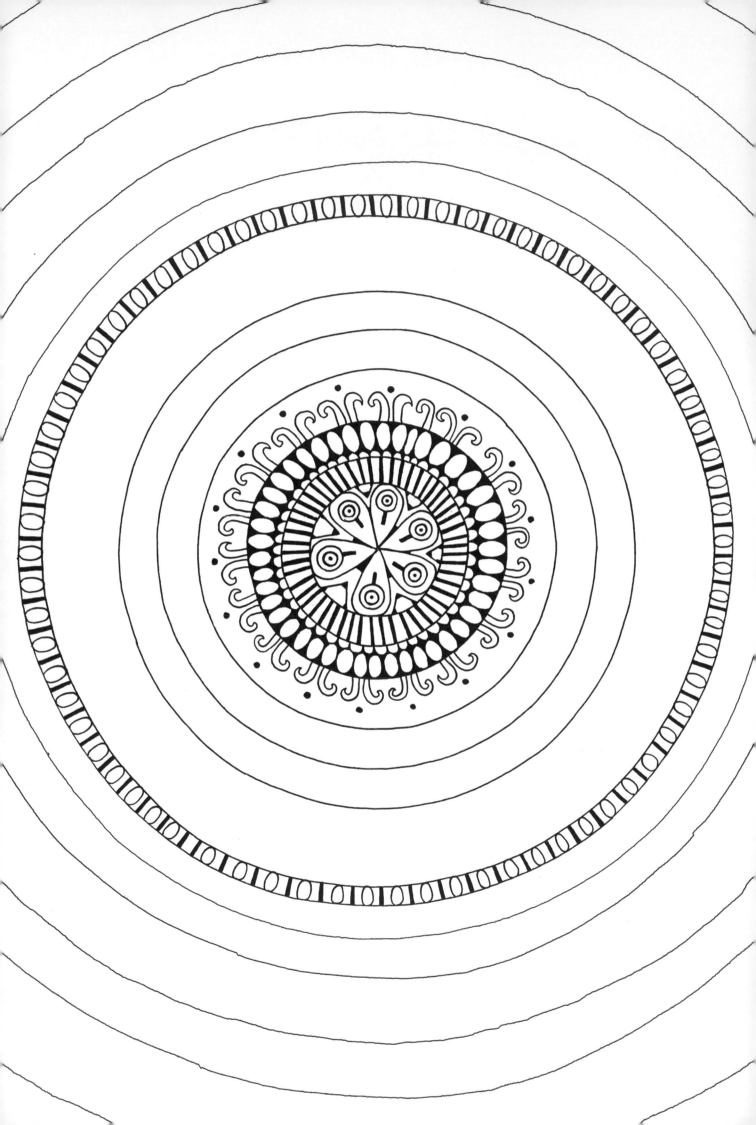

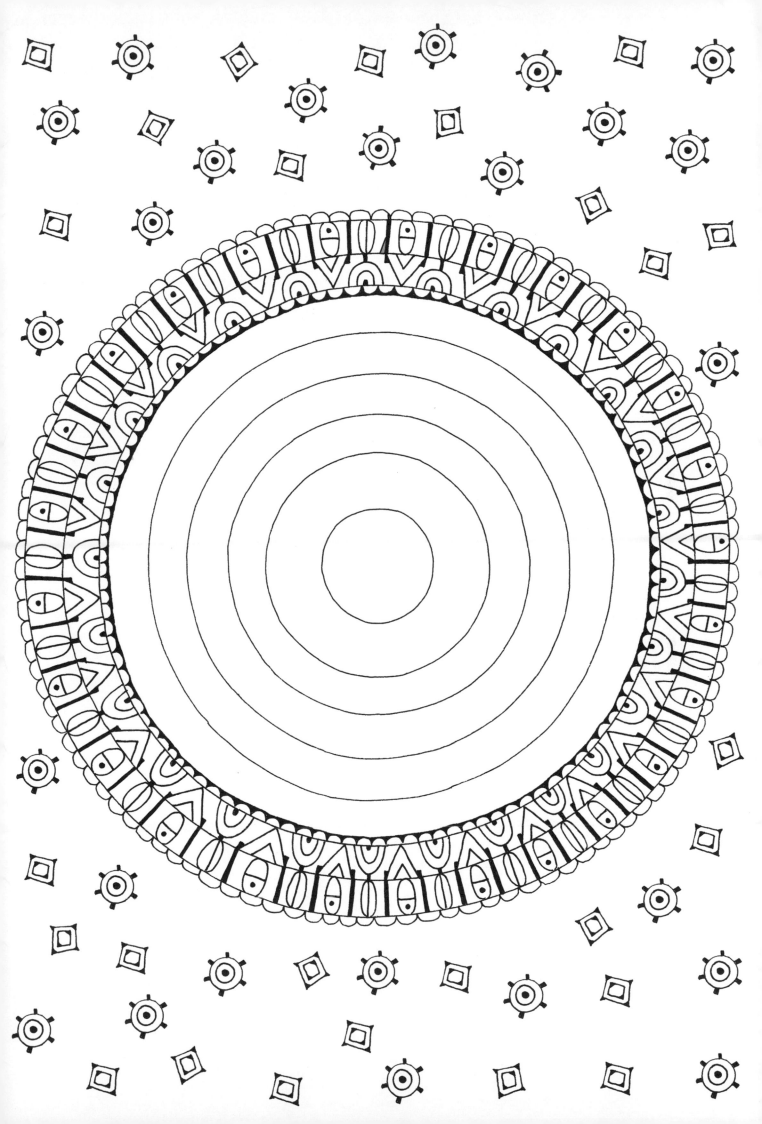

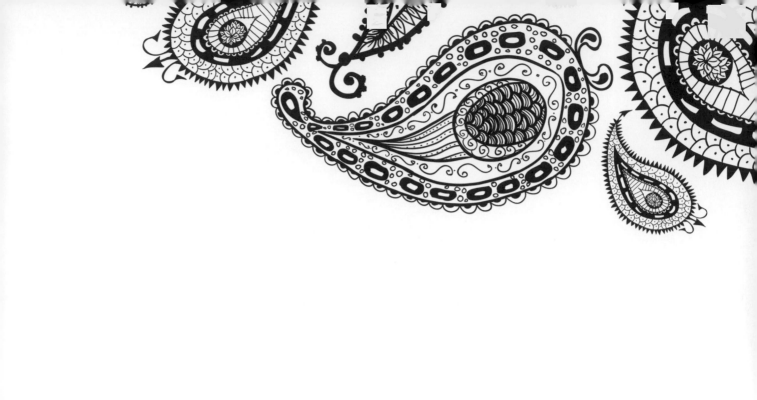
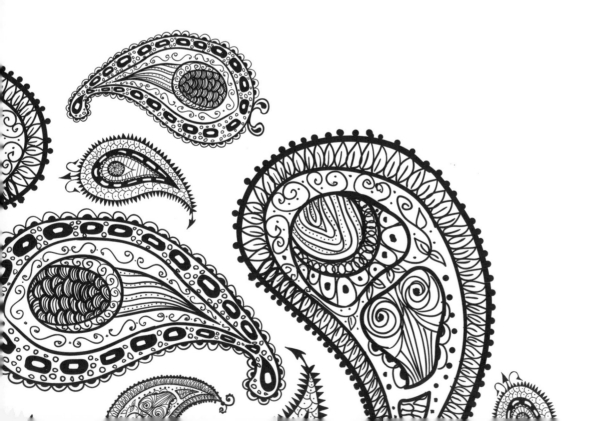

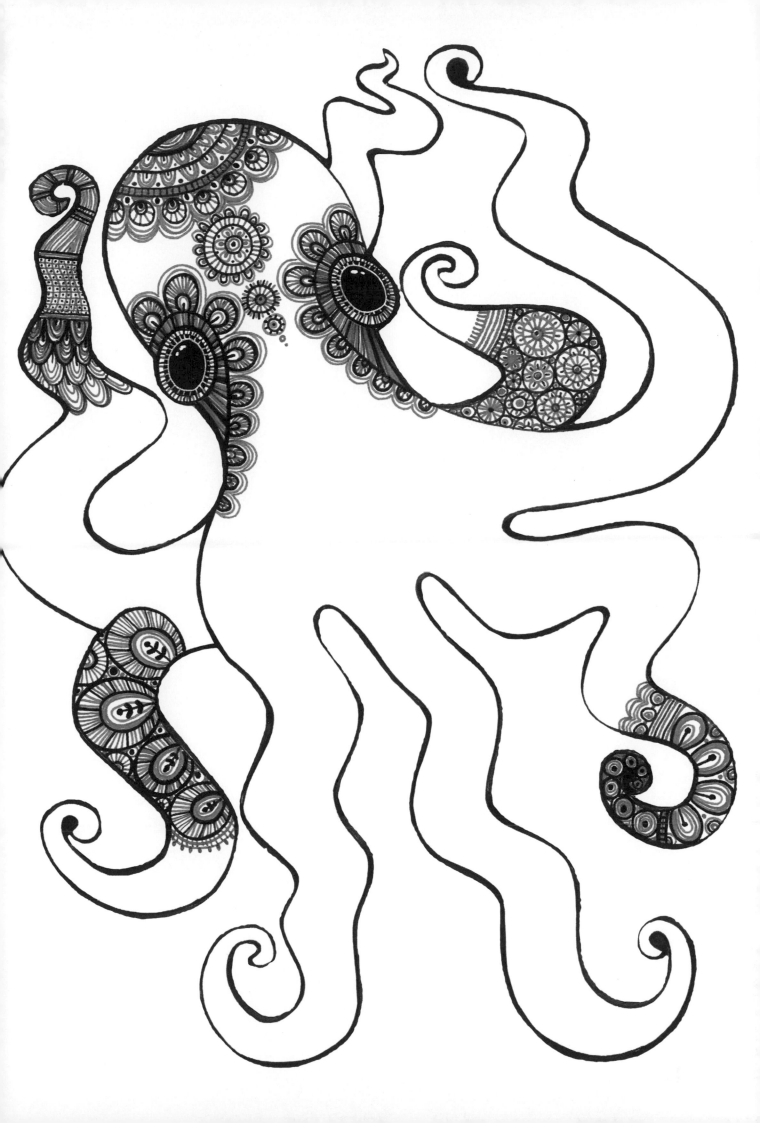

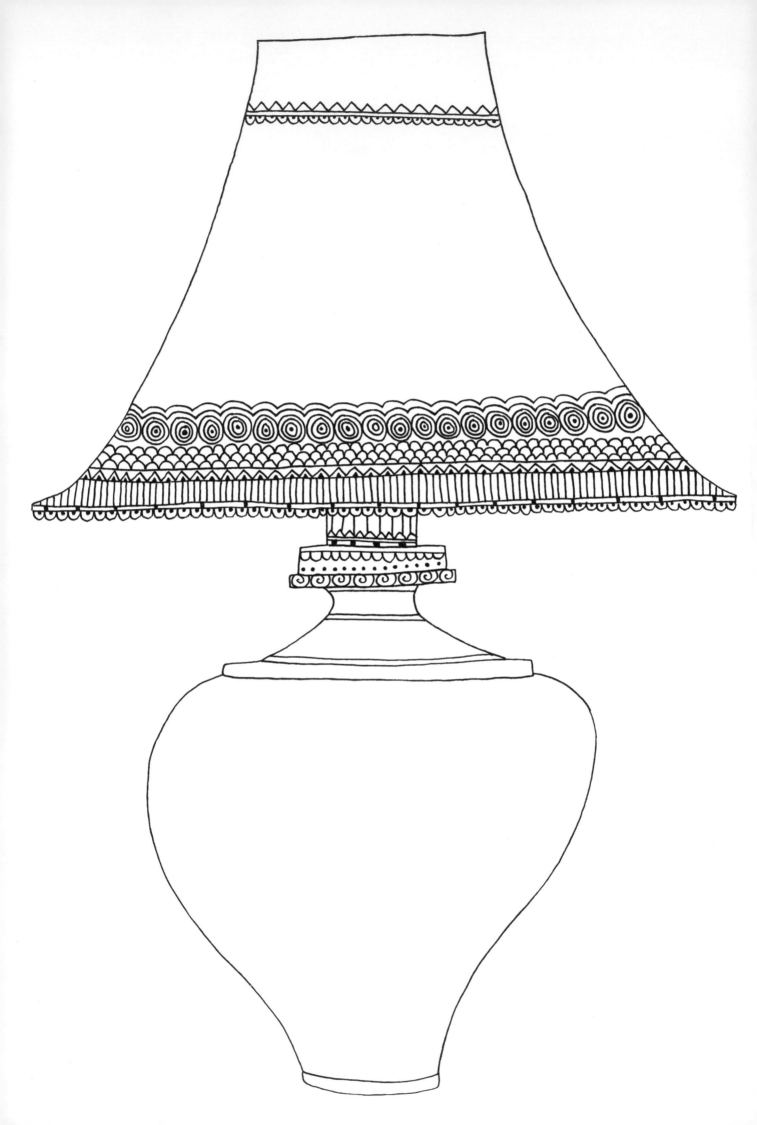

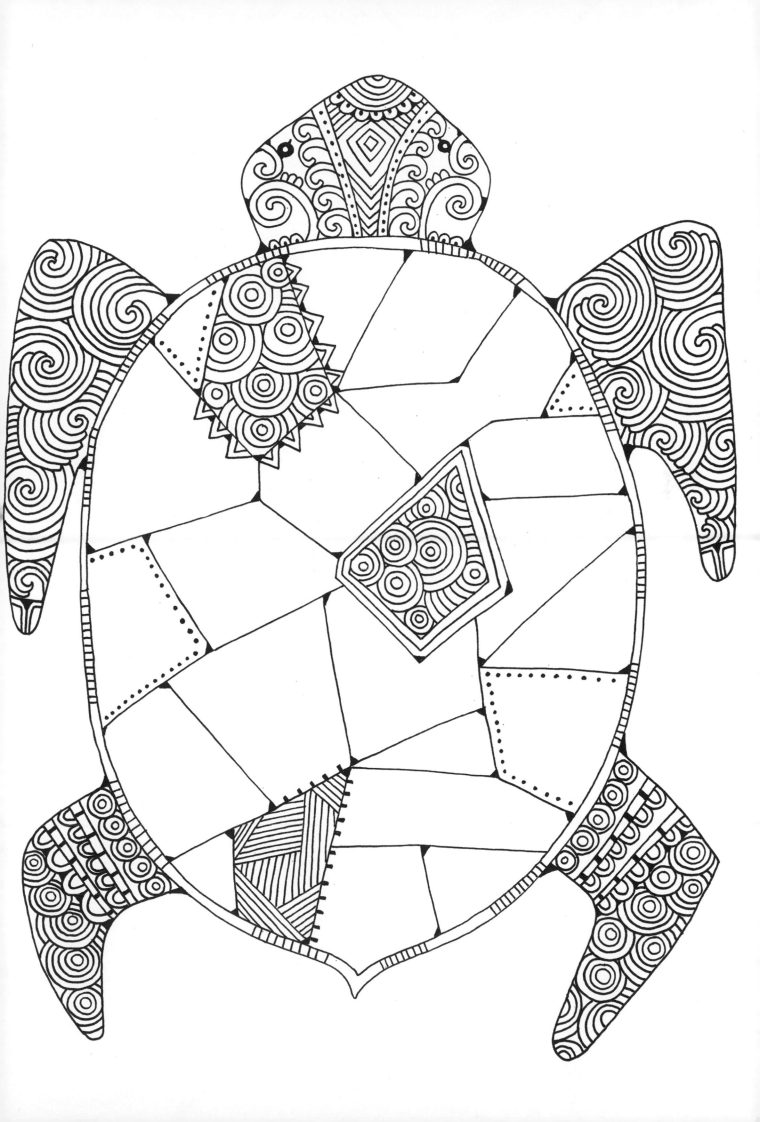

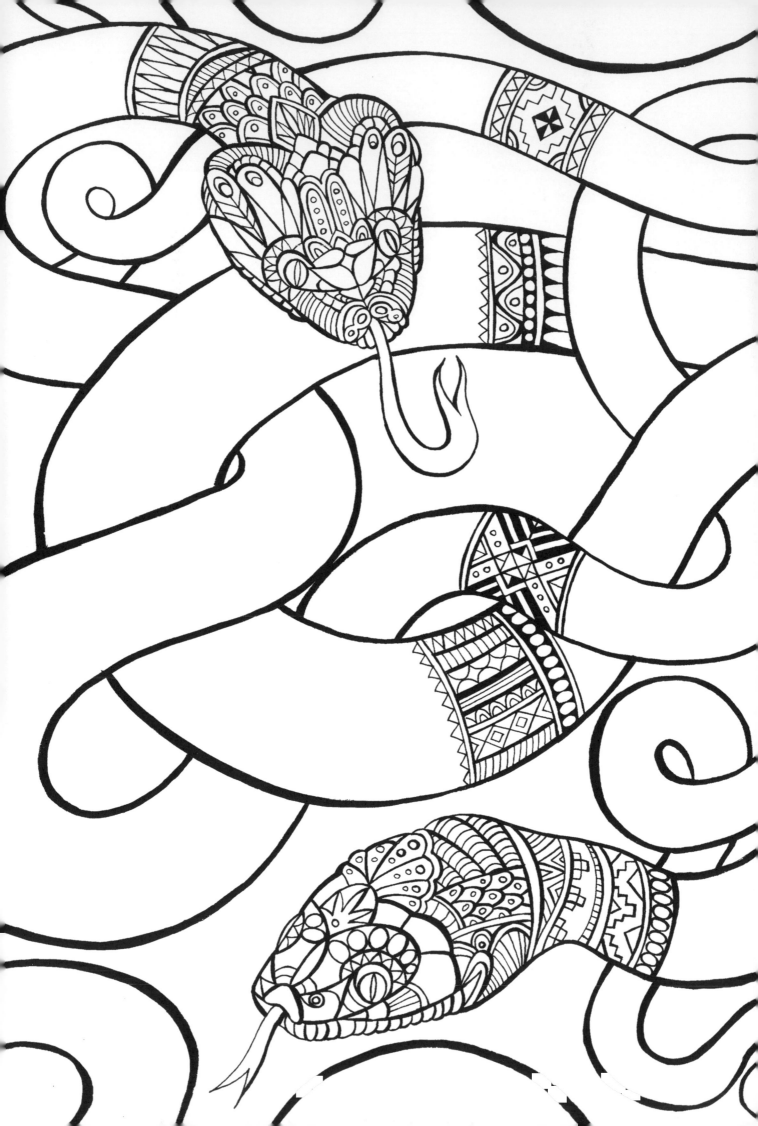

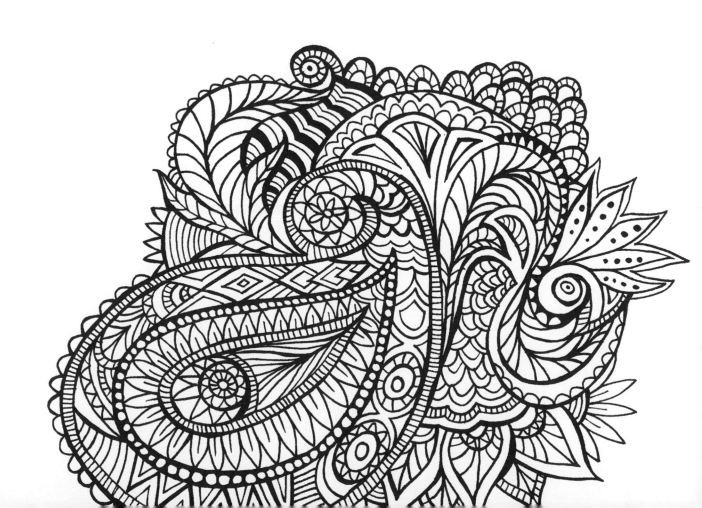

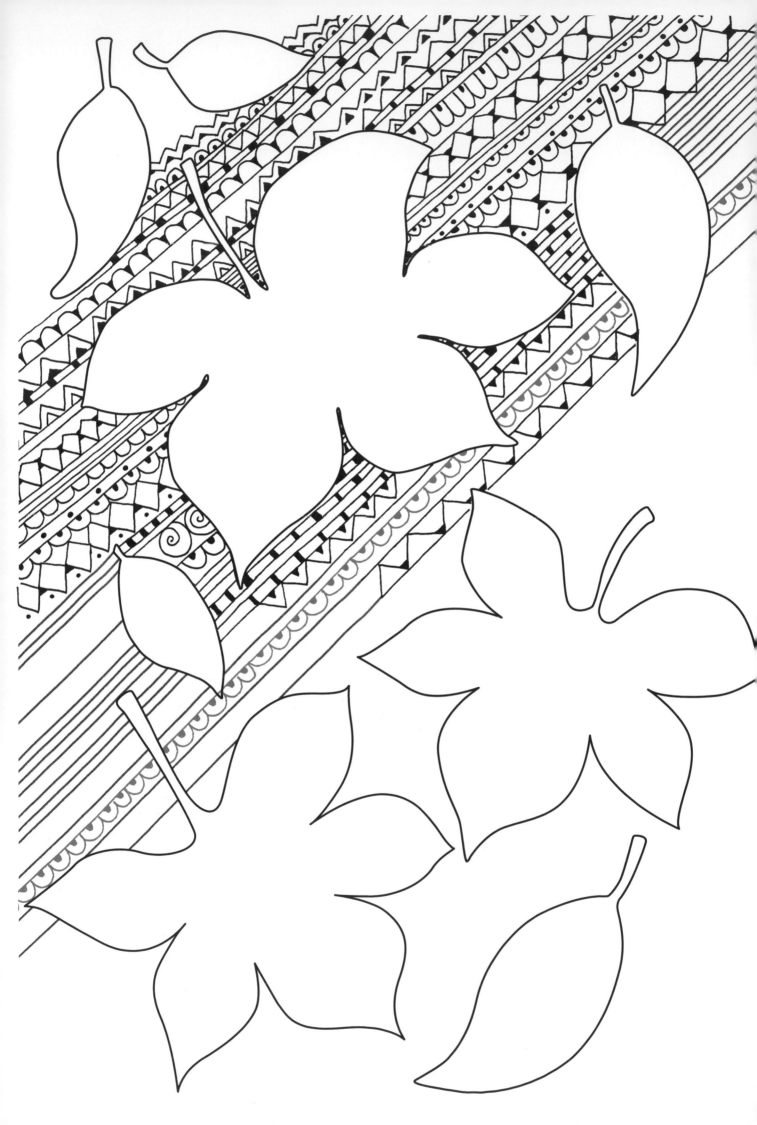

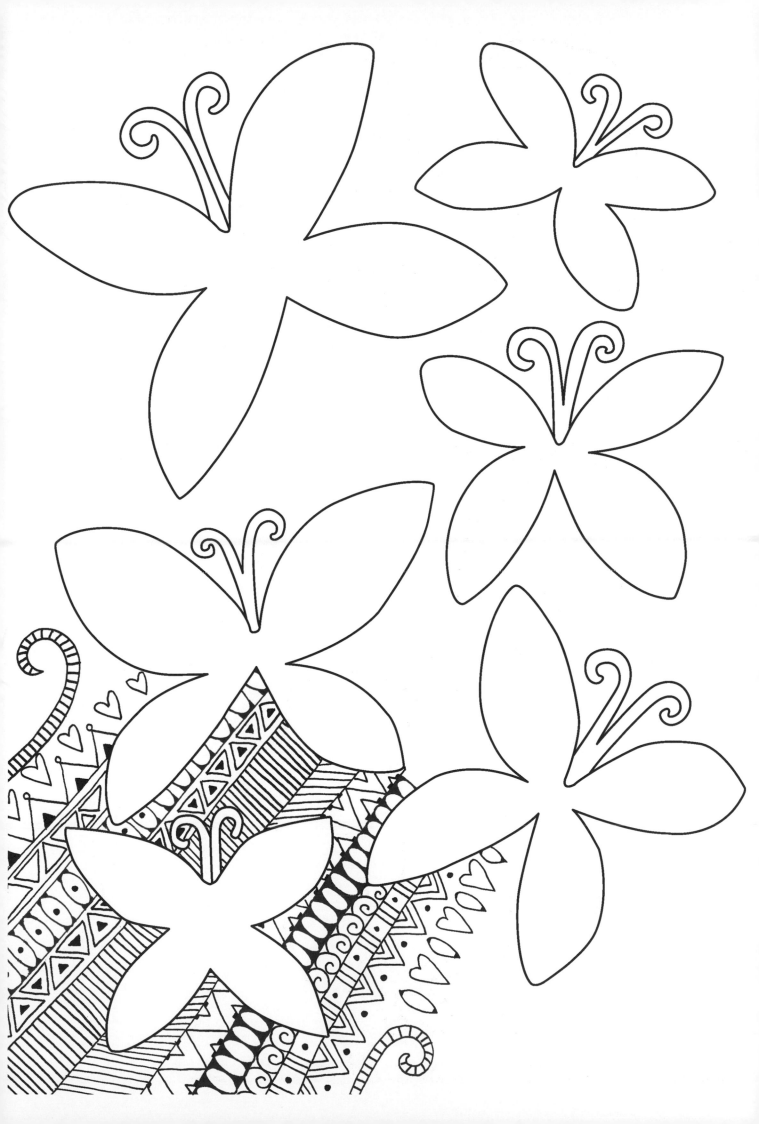

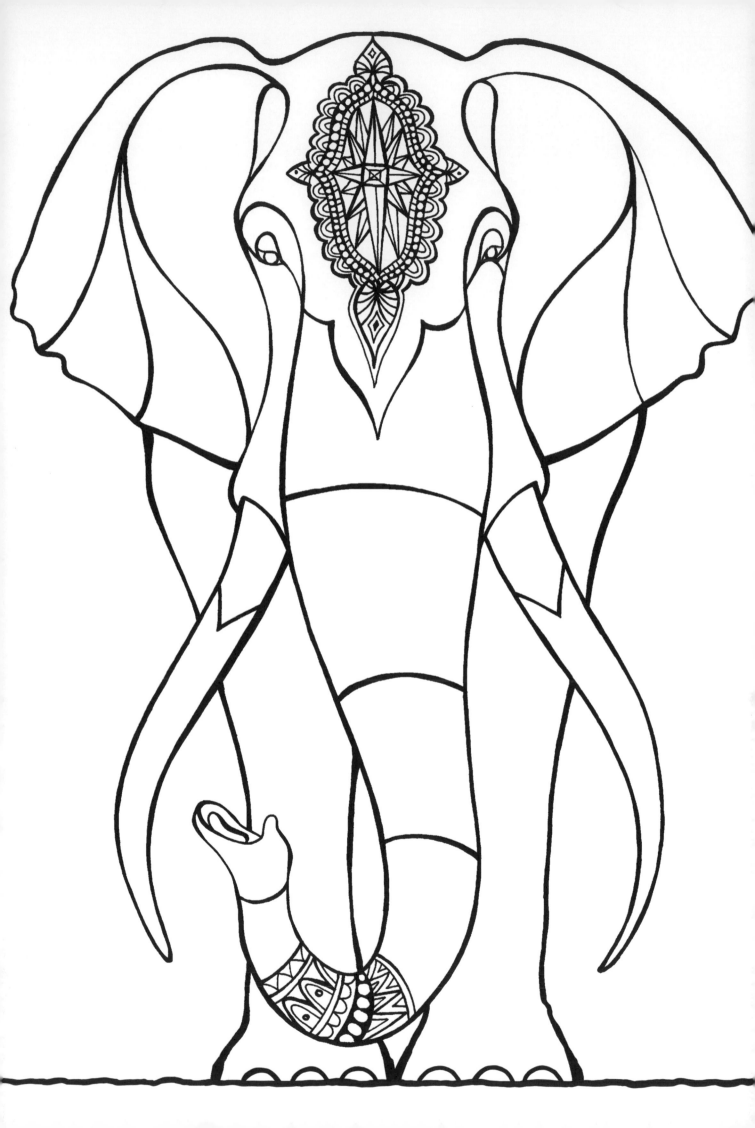

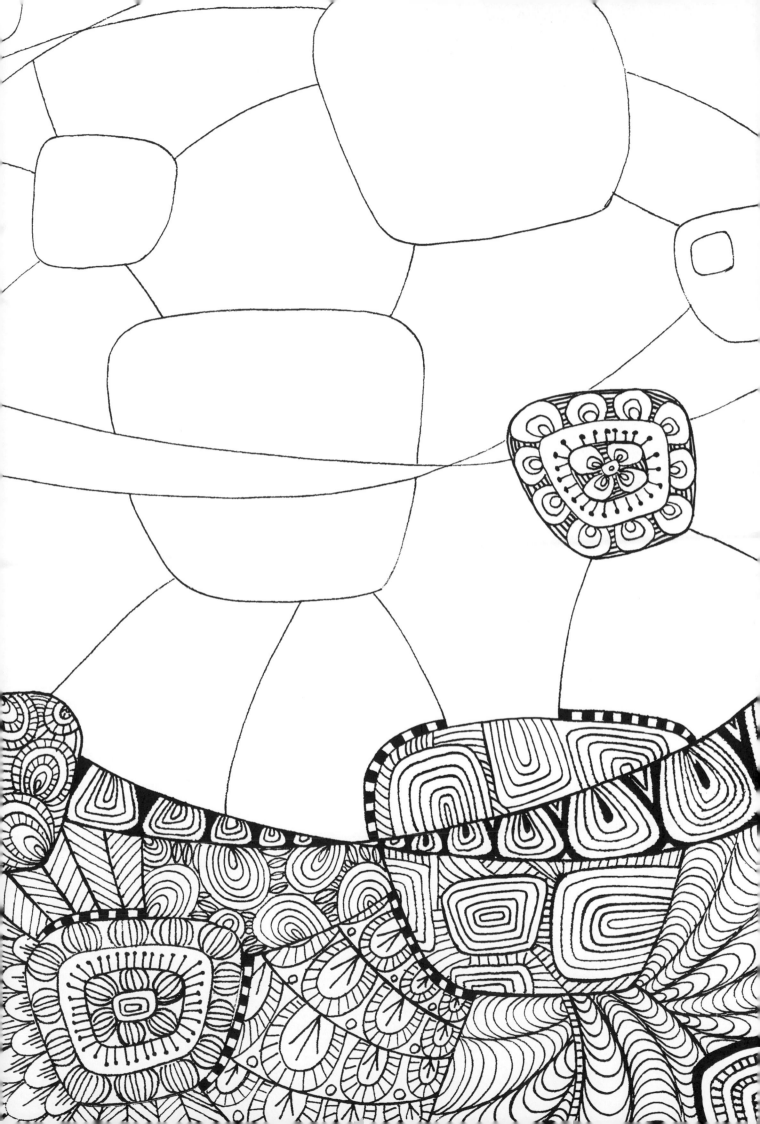

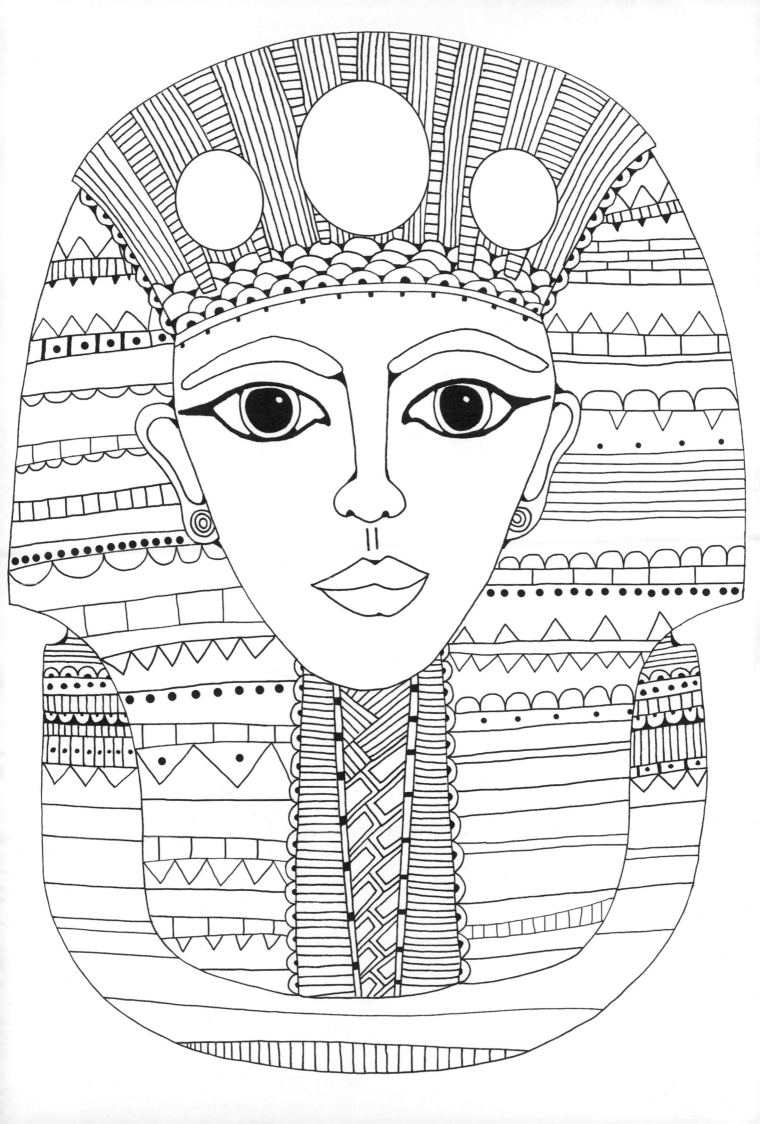

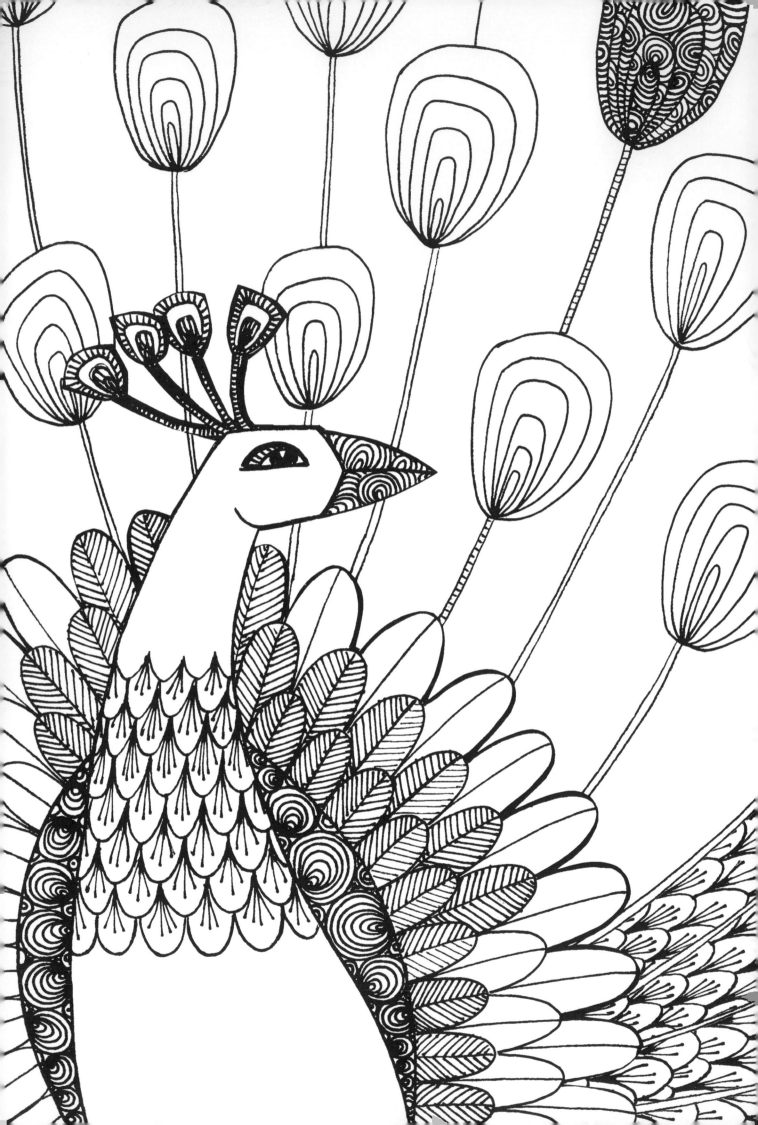

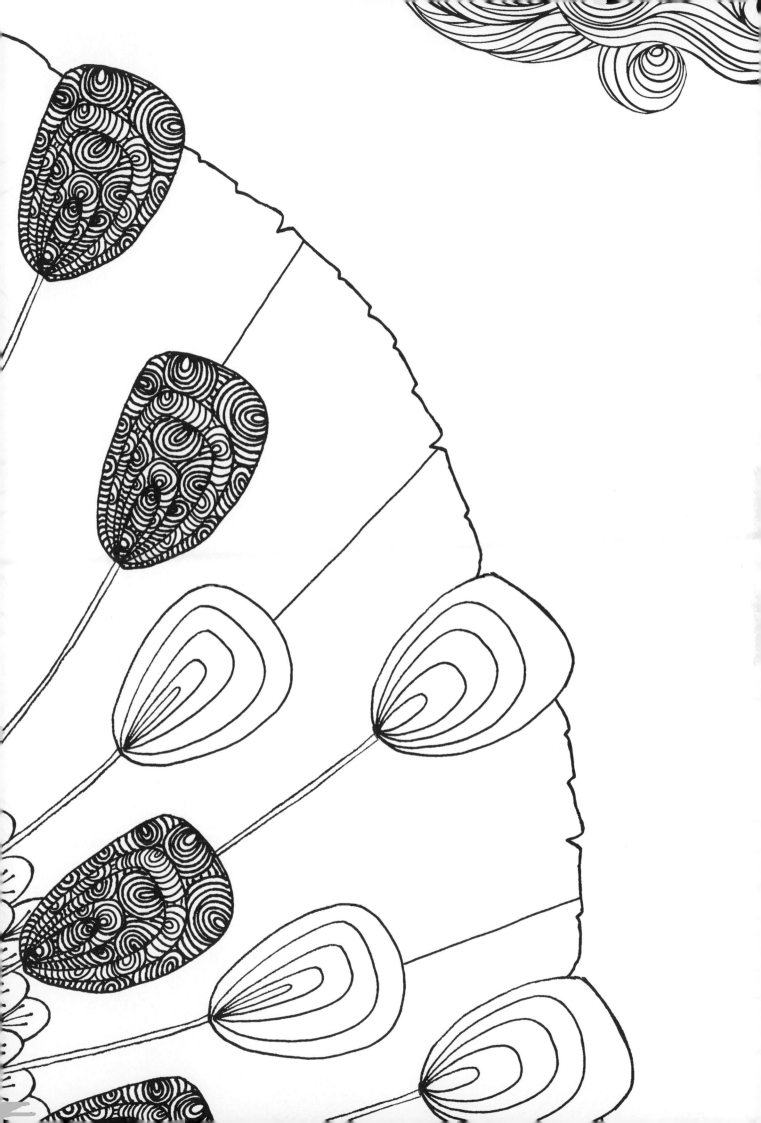

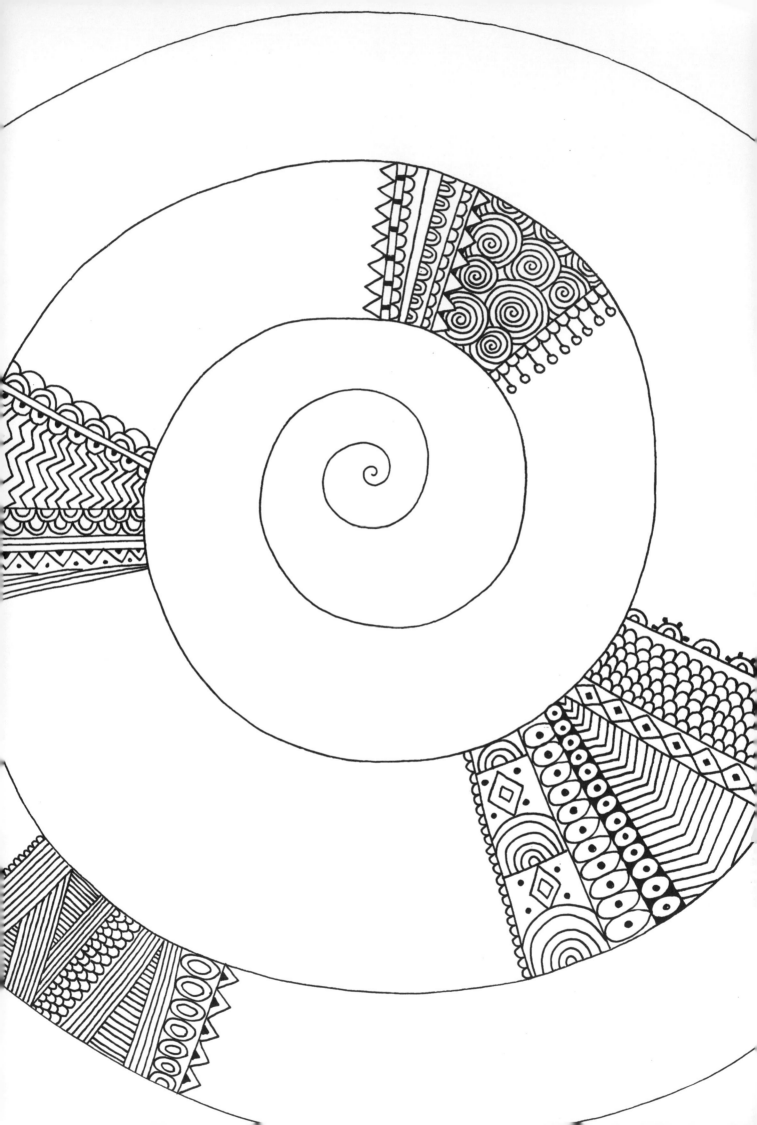

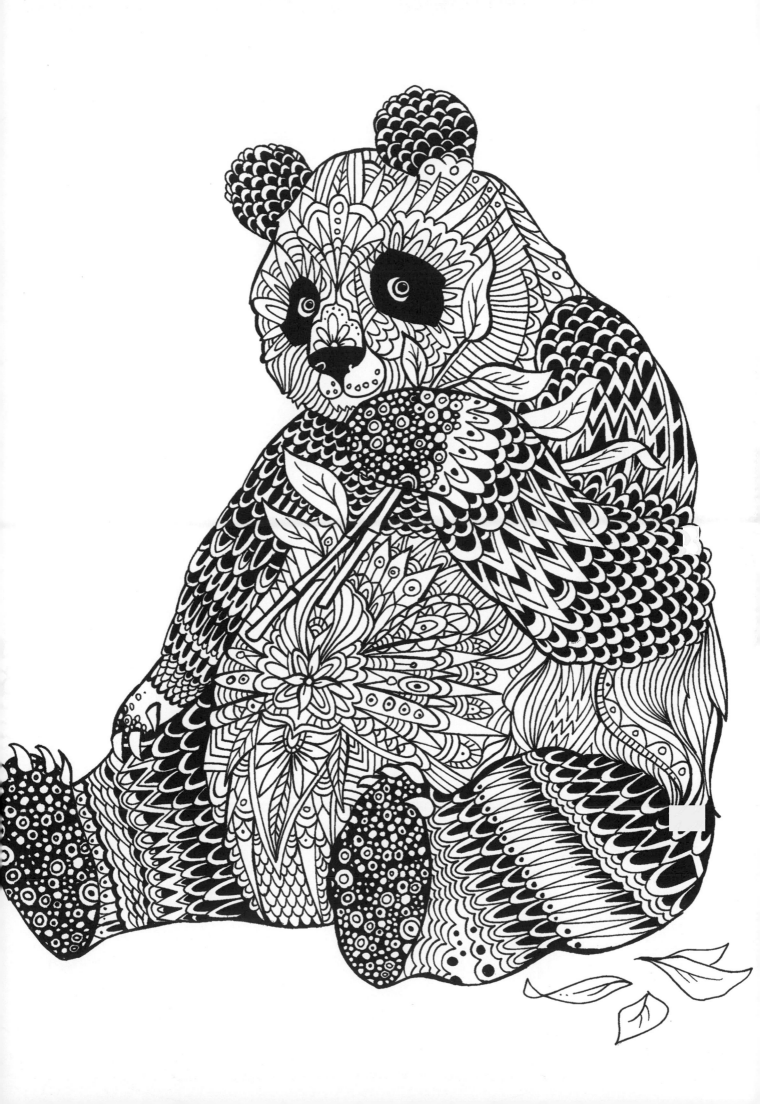

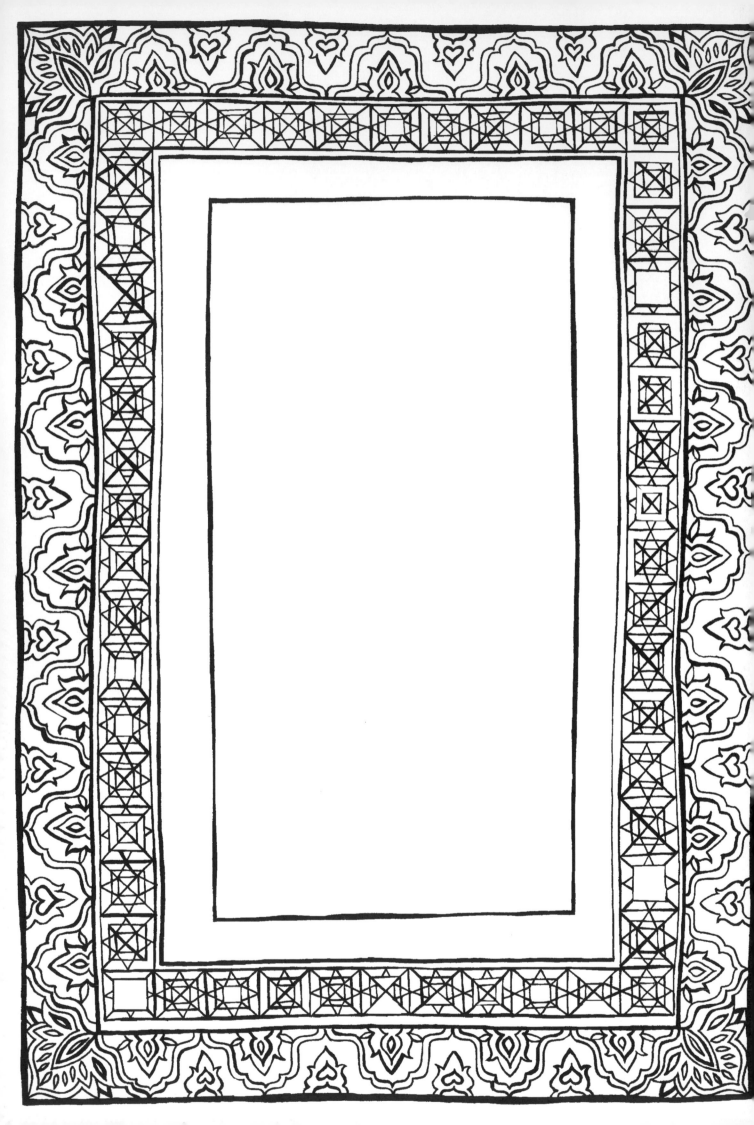

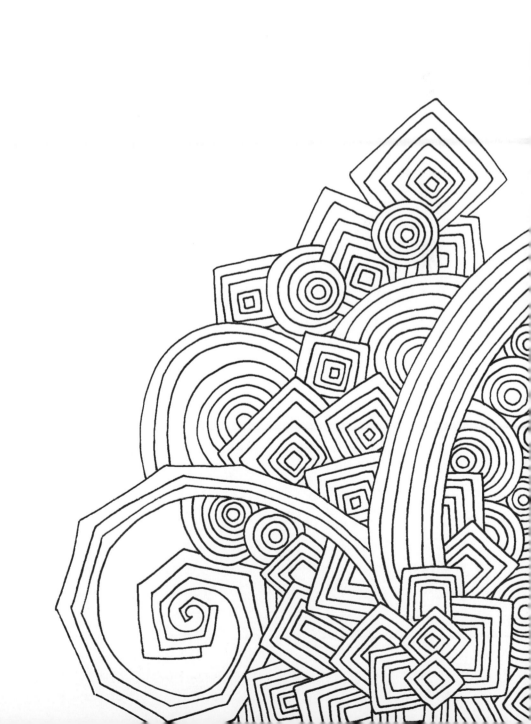

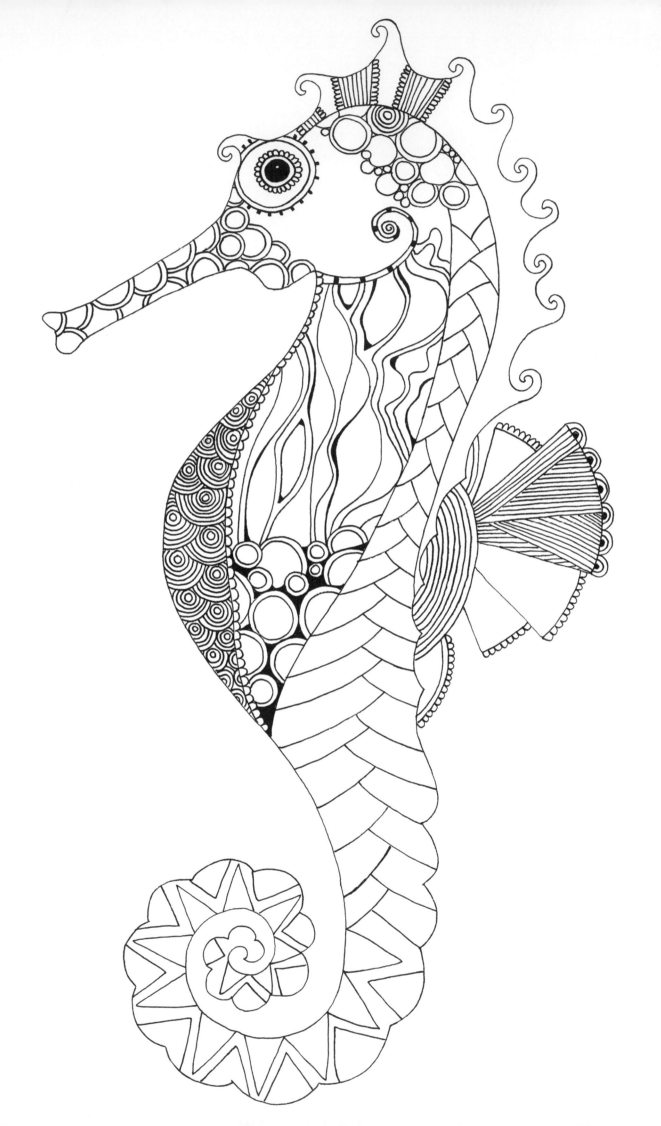

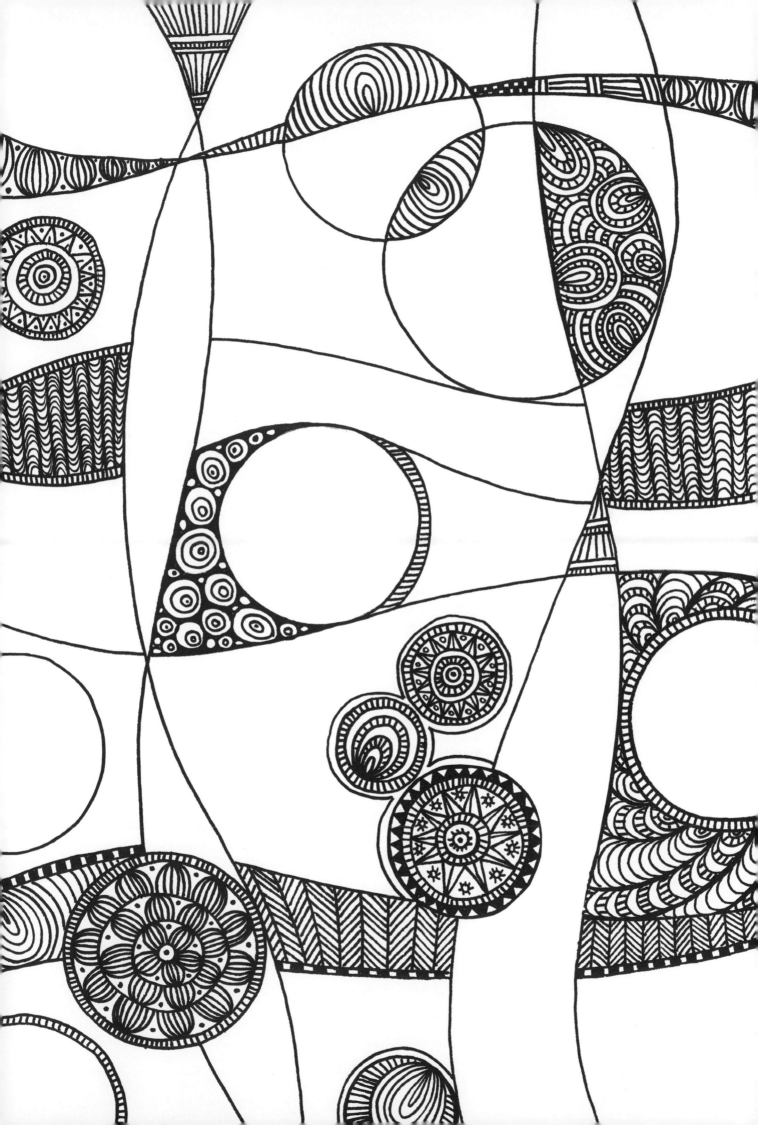

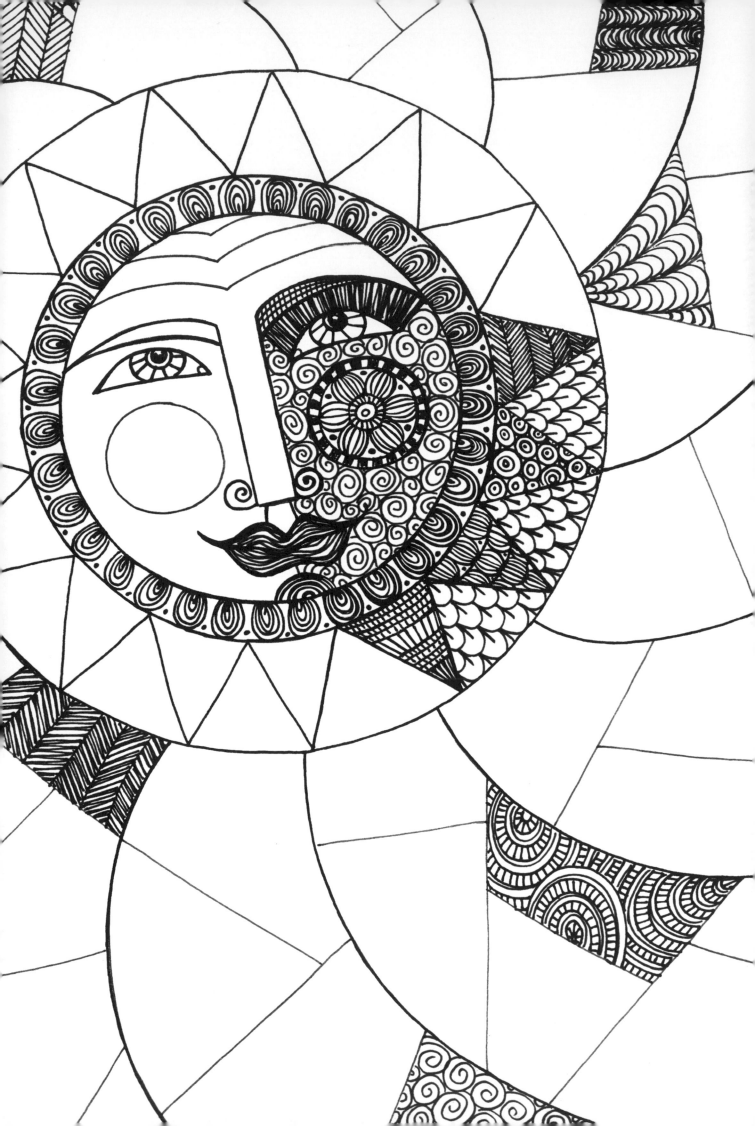

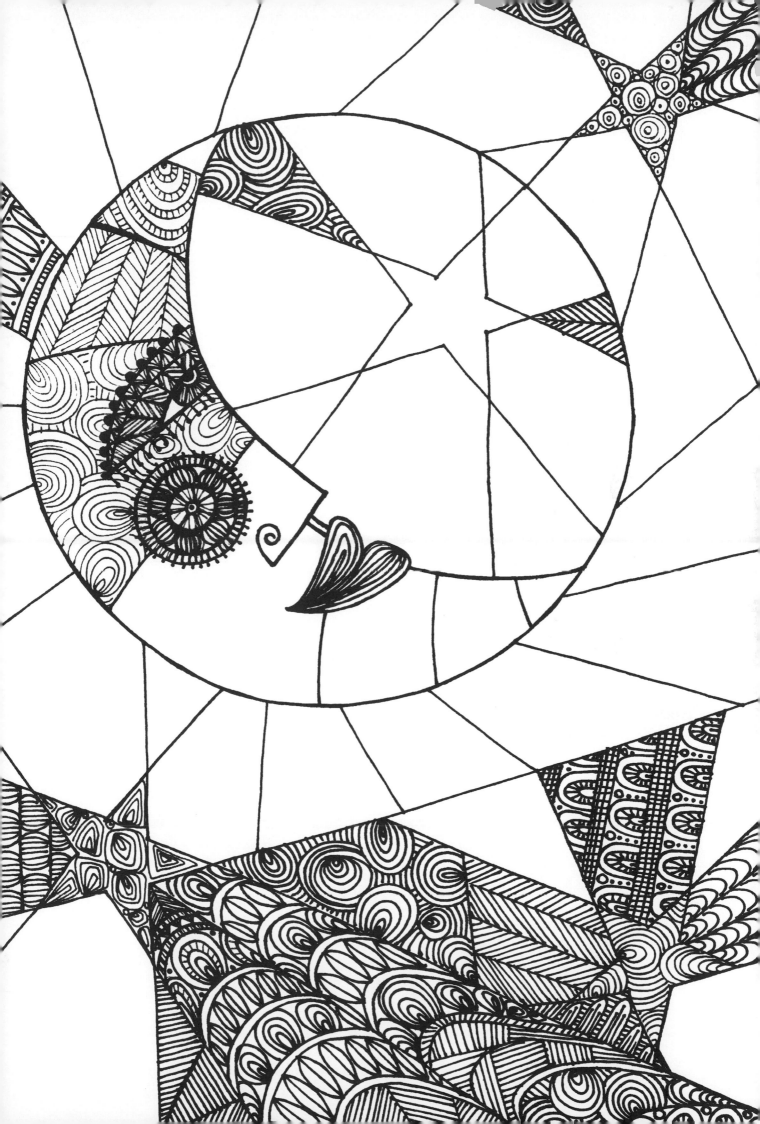

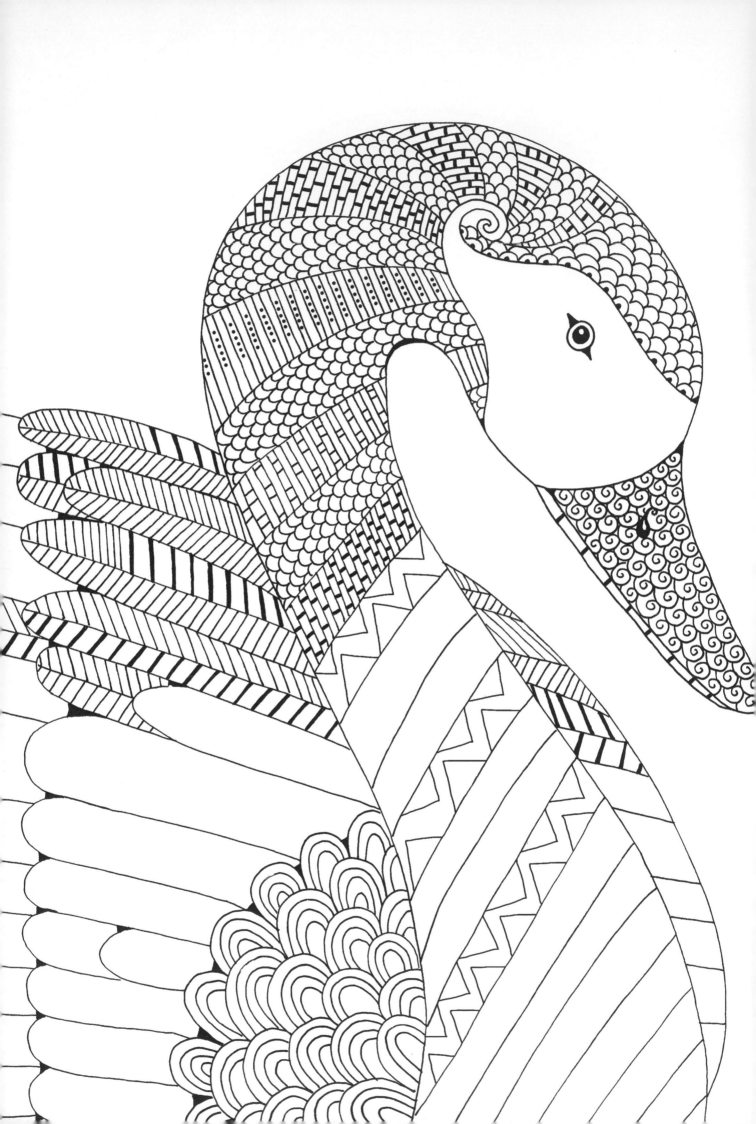

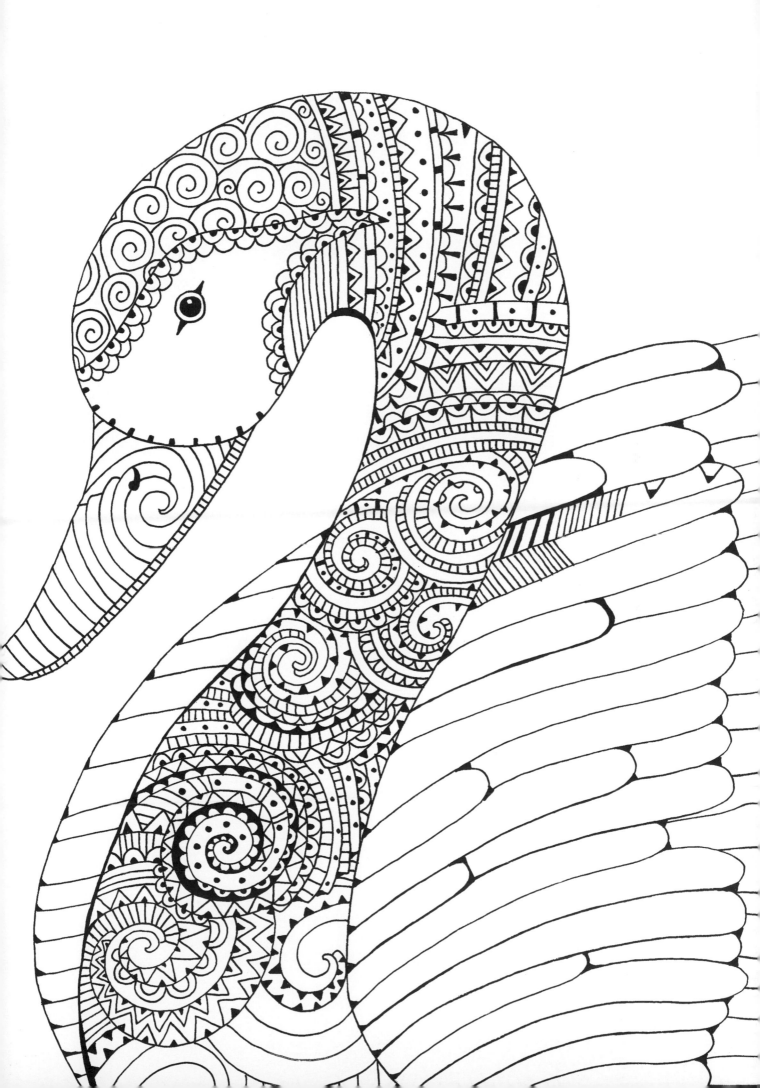

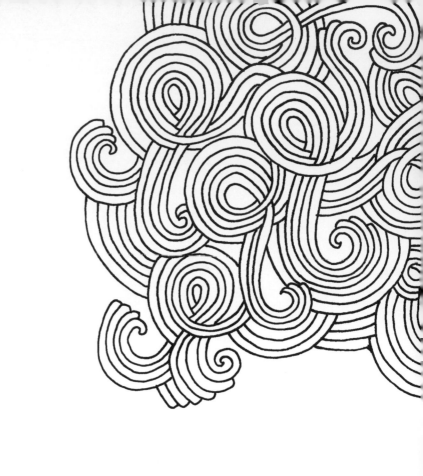

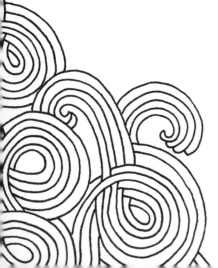

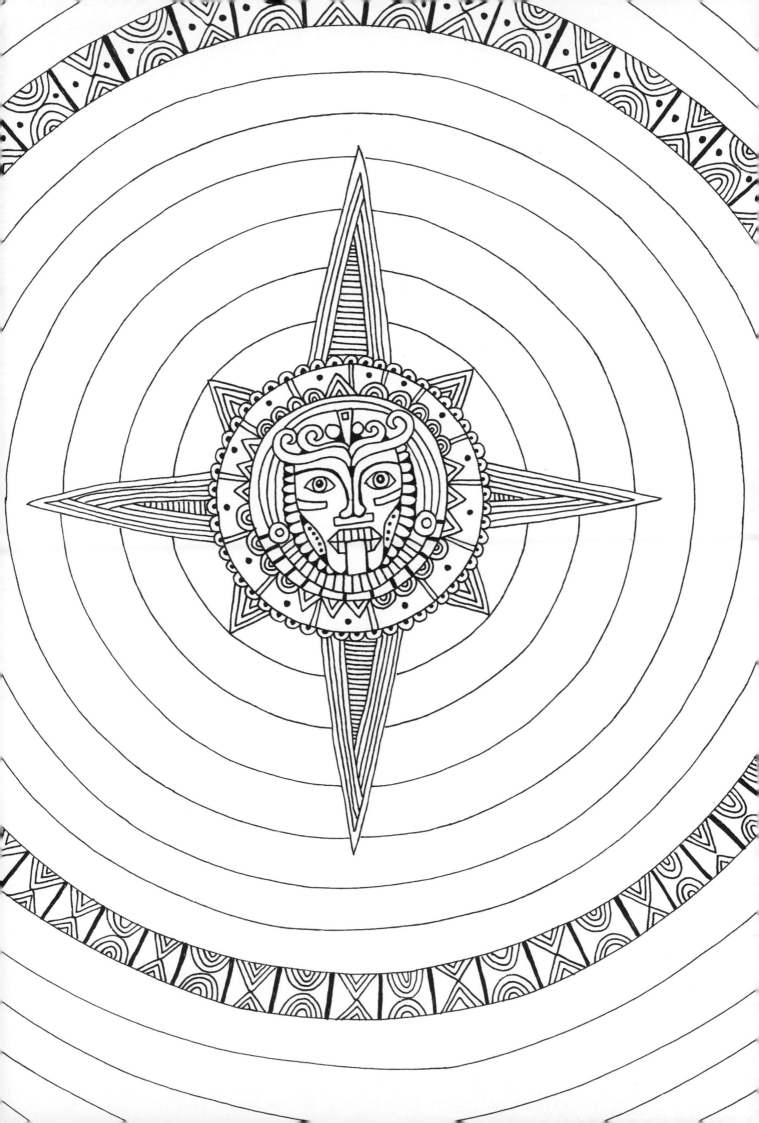

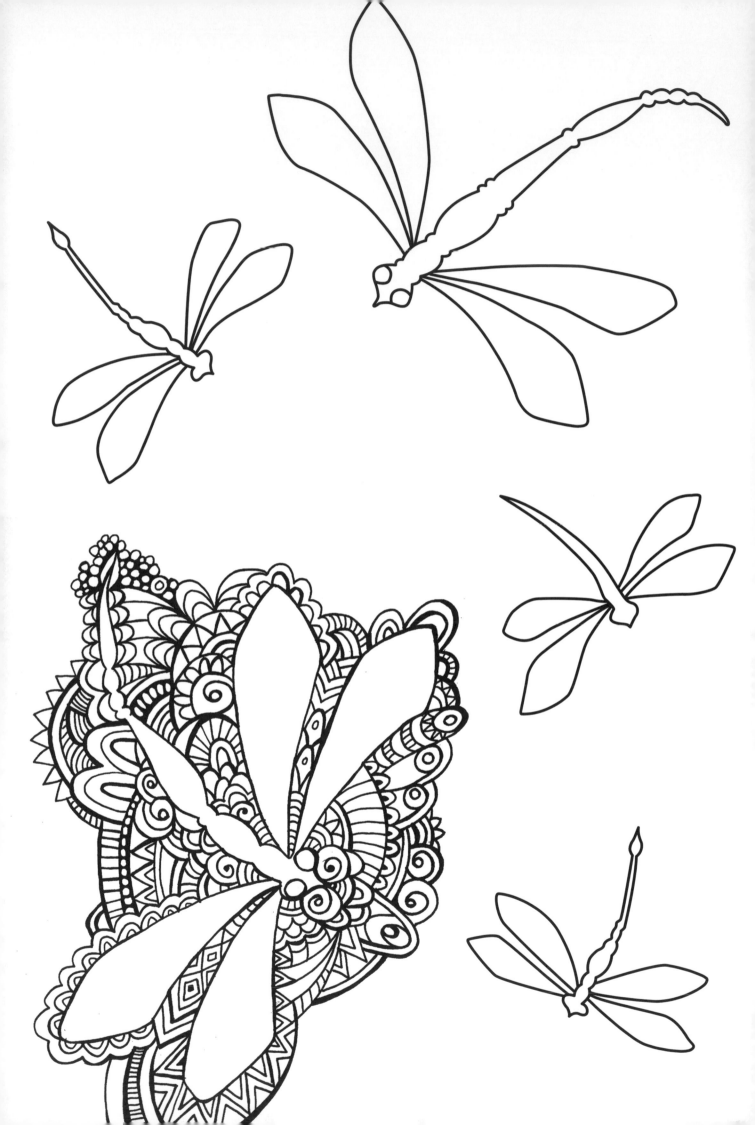

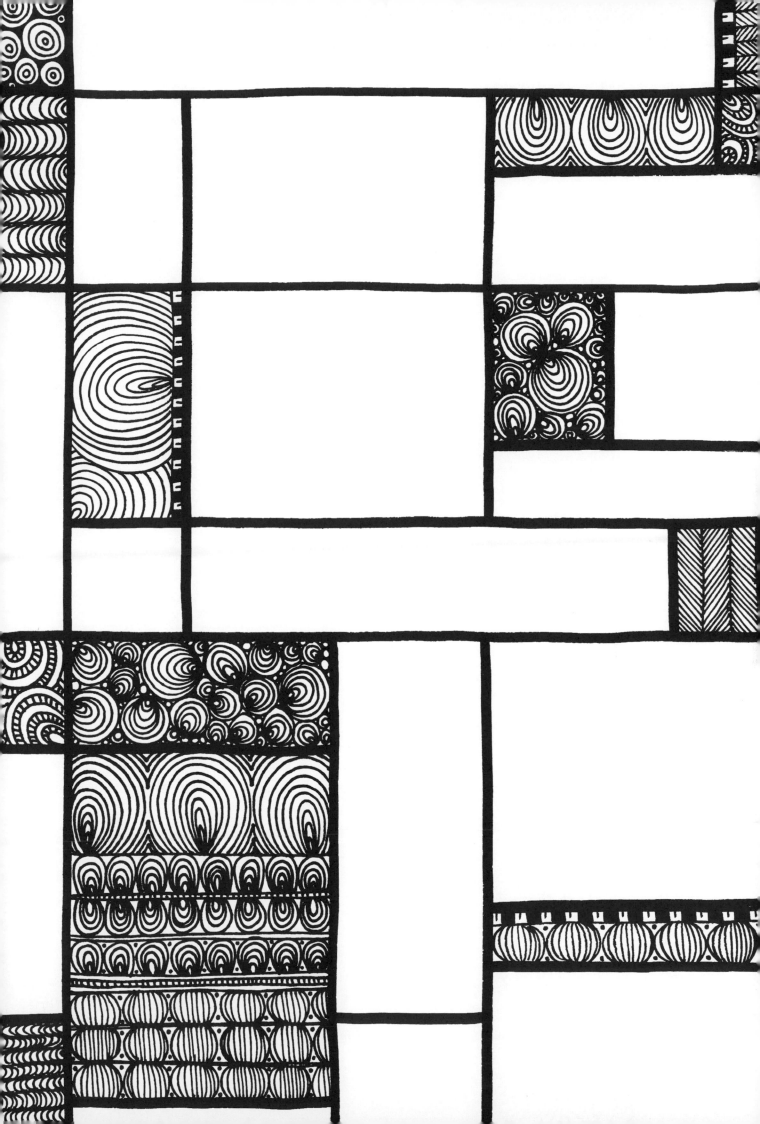

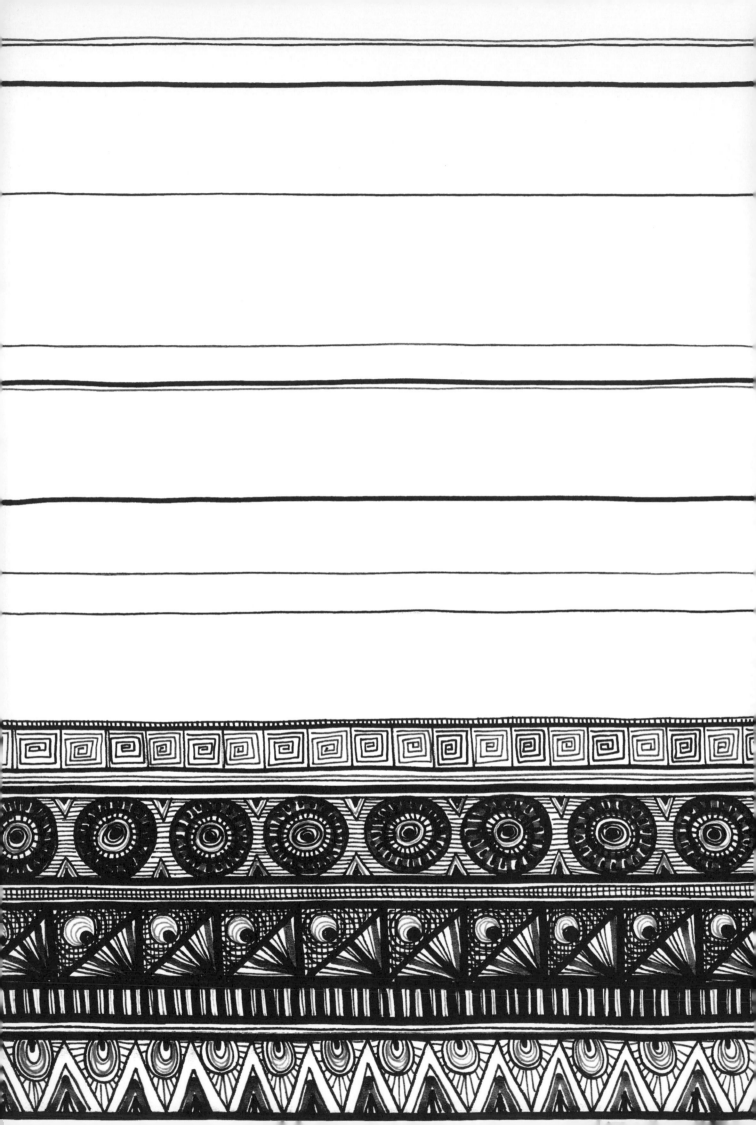

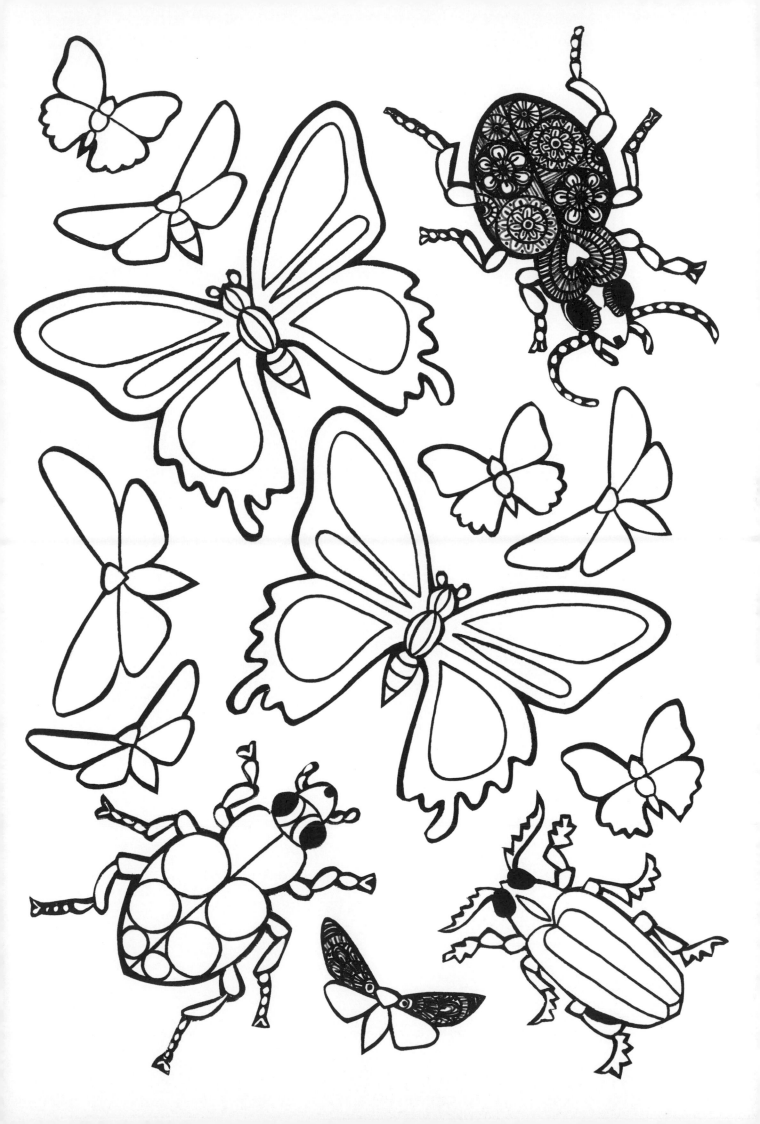

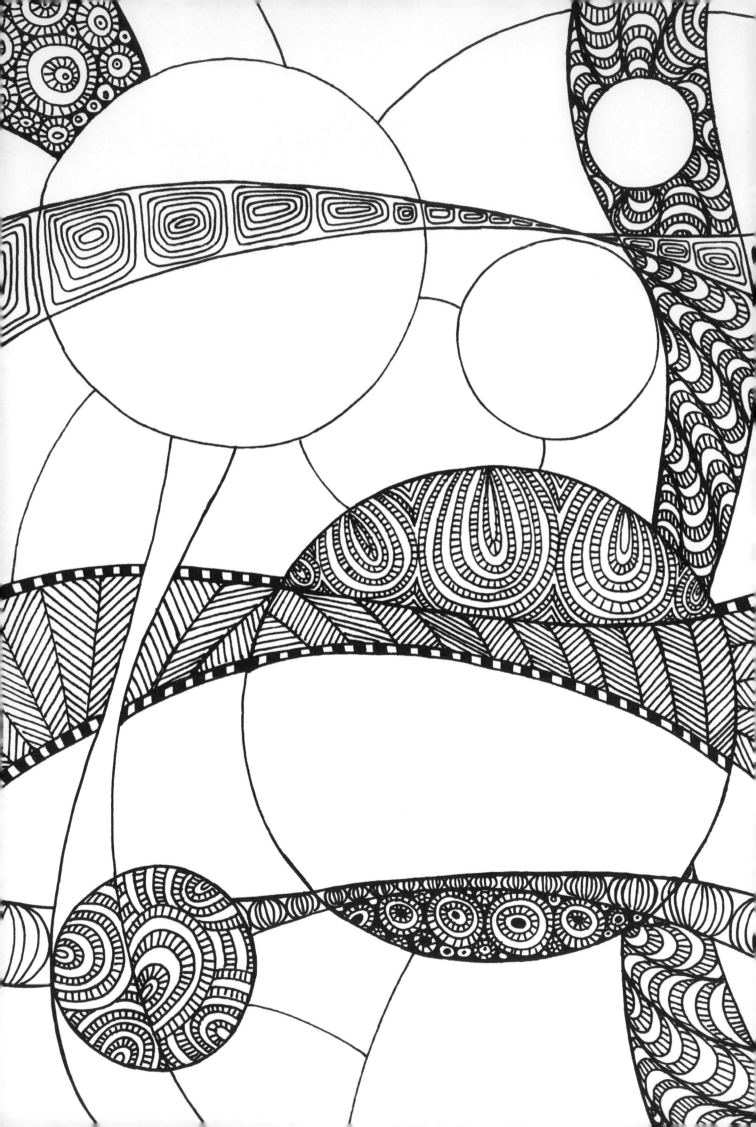

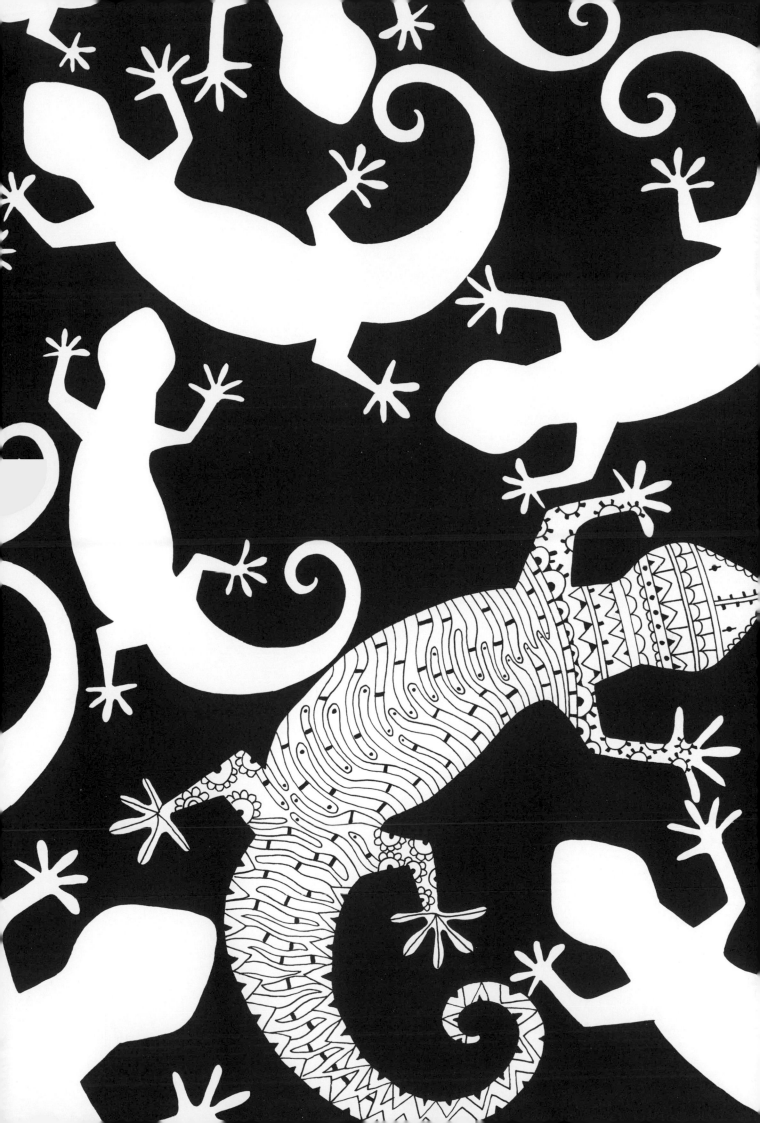

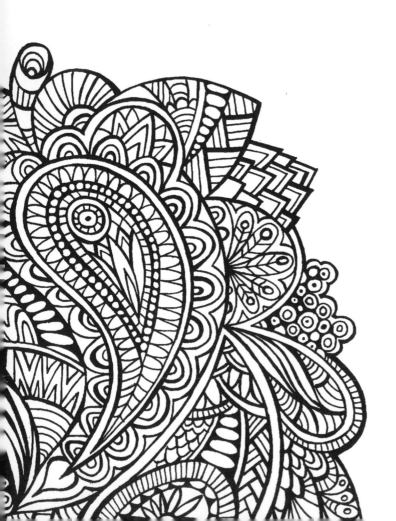

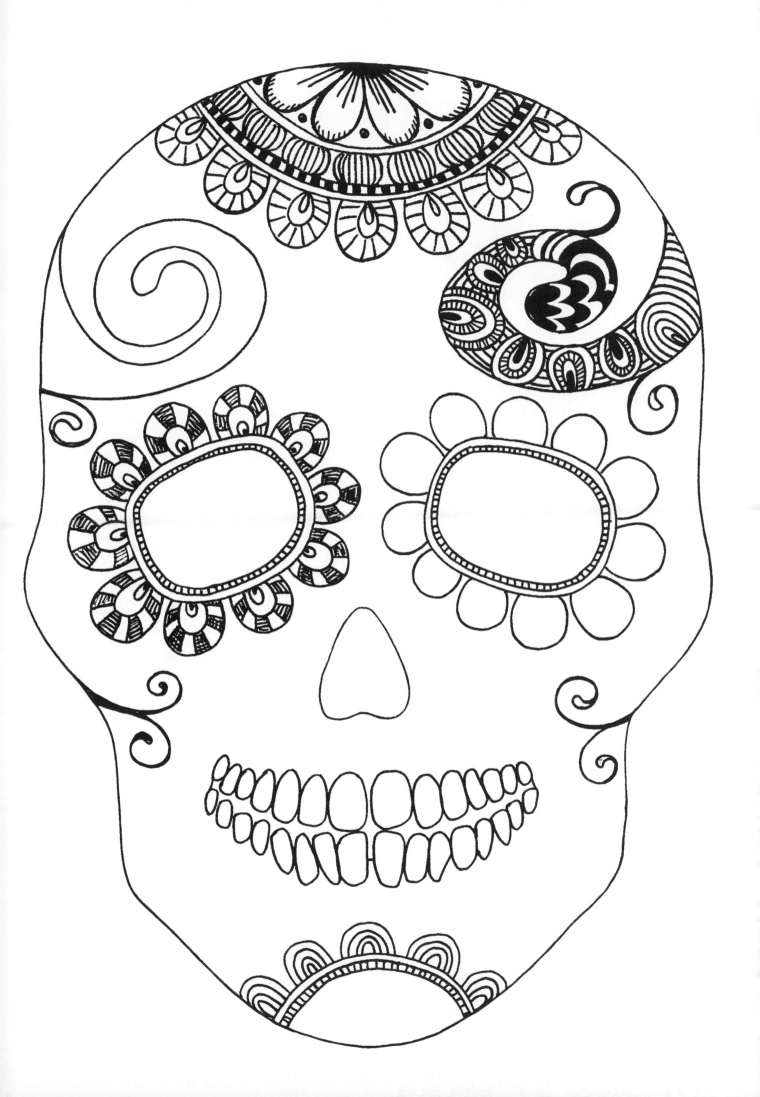

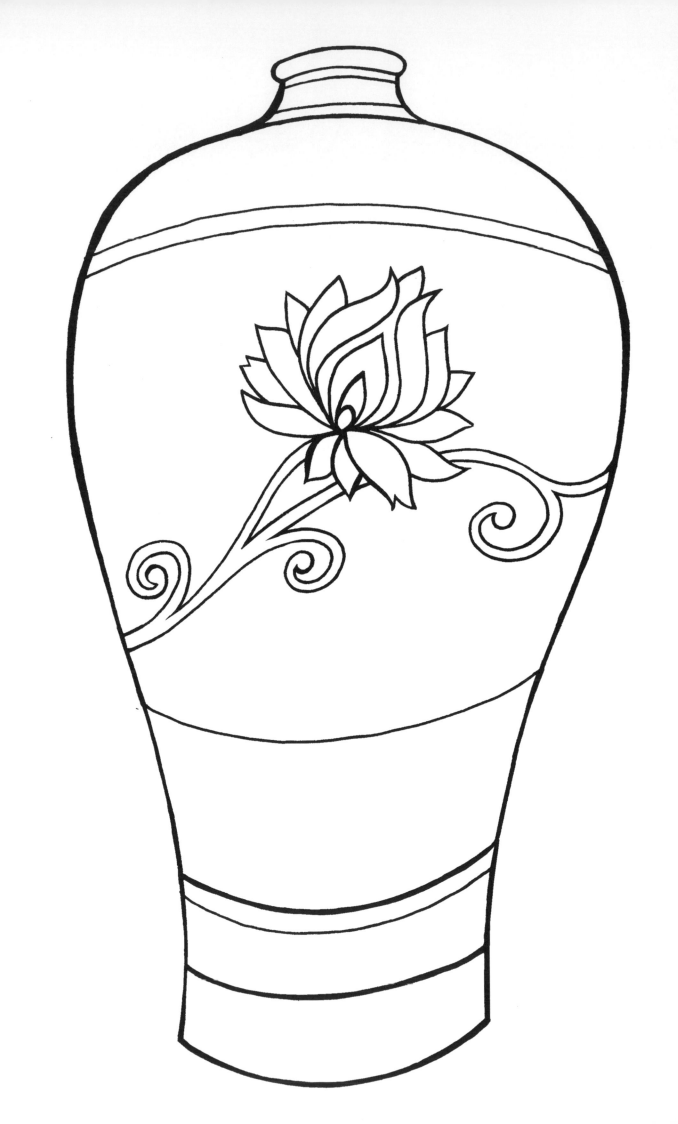

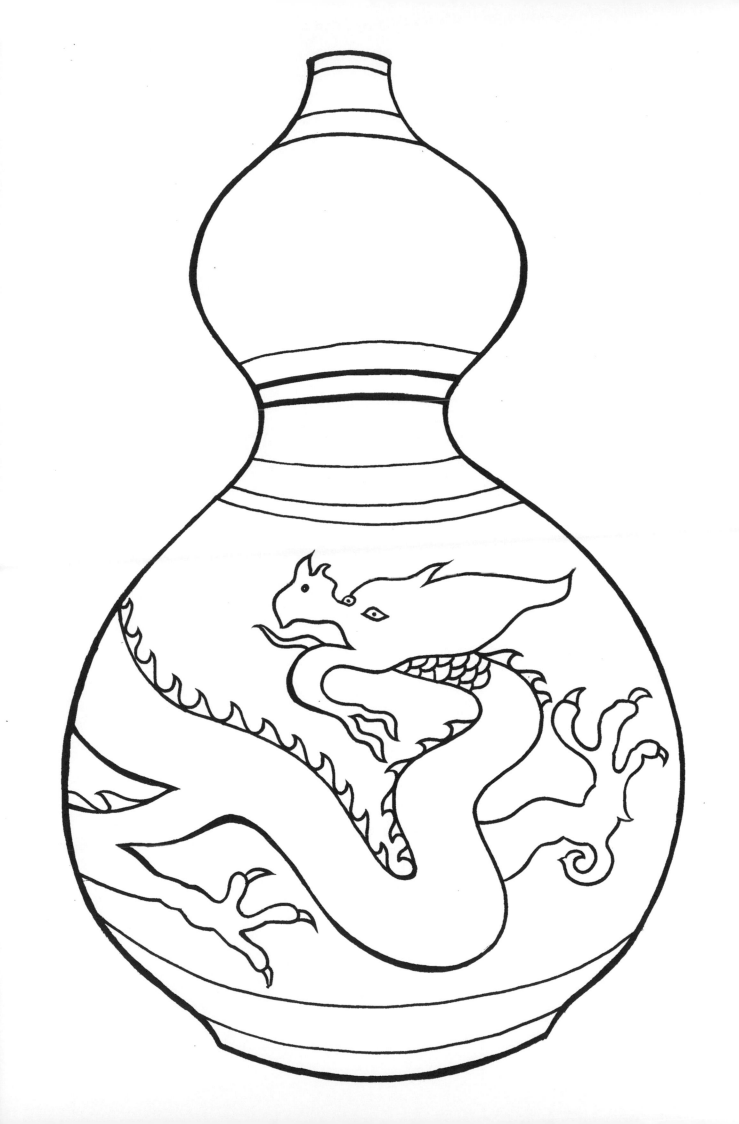

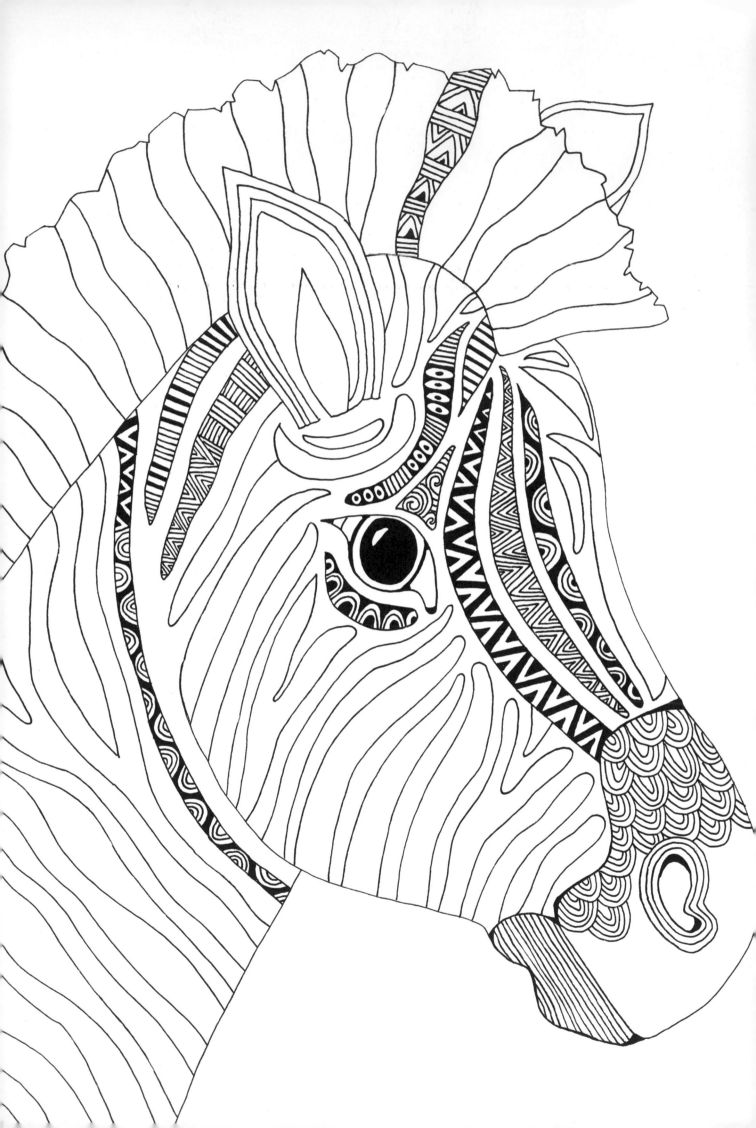